Passive Income Ideas 2020

Includes Dropshipping, FBA, Stock Market Investing, Real Estate, Day Trading, Affiliate Marketing. Strategies for Beginners to Make Money Online with Location & Time Freedom.

© **Copyright 2020 Brook Spencer - All rights reserved.**

The content contained within this book may not be reproduced, duplicated or transmitted without direct written permission from the author or the publisher.

Under no circumstances will any blame or legal responsibility be held against the publisher, or author, for any damages, reparation, or monetary loss due to the information contained within this book. Either directly or indirectly.

Legal Notice:

This book is copyright protected. This book is only for personal use. You cannot amend, distribute, sell, use, quote or paraphrase any part, or the content within this book, without the consent of the author or publisher.

Disclaimer Notice:

Please note the information contained within this document is for educational and entertainment purposes only. All effort has been executed to present accurate, up to date, and reliable, complete information. No warranties of any kind are declared or implied. Readers acknowledge that the author is not engaging in the rendering of legal, financial, medical or professional advice. The content within this book has been derived from various sources. Please consult a licensed professional before attempting any techniques outlined in this book.

By reading this document, the reader agrees that under no circumstances is the author responsible for any losses, direct or indirect, which are incurred as a result of the use of information contained within this document, including, but not limited to, — errors, omissions, or inaccuracies.

Introduction	6
Chapter 1 Understanding Passive Income	11
The Truth About Passive Income	16
What Passive Income Isn't	18
What Passive Income IS	19
Residual vs Passive Income	21
Sources of Passive Income	26
Chapter 2 Kindle-Publishing	39
How to Make It Work for You	41
Marketing with Kindle Publishing	41
Chapter 3 Amazon FBA	45
Ratings Based on Our Criteria	47
Tips for Success	49
FAQs	51
Myth Busters About Amazon FBA	58
Chapter 4 Affiliate Marketing	60
Benefits of Affiliate Marketing	60
How You Earn Money This Way	61
Getting Started With Affiliate Marketing	62

Choosing Your Niche	62
Building Your Audience	63
Finding Affiliate Programs	65

Chapter 5 Dropshipping — 67

How to Start Drop shipping Successfully — 69

Chapter 6 Retail arbitrage — 74

Chapter 7 Cryptocurrency — 80

Tips for Success — 82

Chapter 8 Stock Market — 84

Chapter 9 Option Trading — 90

What is an option? — 91

Options Expire — 92

Pricing definitions — 94

Writing, Buying, and Selling — 96

Maximum Financial Risk — 97

Pros and Cons of Options Trading — 98

Chapter 10 Dividend Investing — 102

How Dividend Investing Can Fit into Your Retirement Goals — 105

Chapter 11 Real estate — 111

Benefits of Real Estate — 111

How You Earn Money Through Real Estate	*112*
Getting Started With Real Estate	*113*
Chapter 12 Domain Flipping	**118**
Getting Started	*119*
Finding the Right Domain	*119*
Chapter 13 Artistry/Creativity	**122**
Chapter 14 Virtual Assistant	**135**
Chapter 15 Online Courses	**140**
Benefits of Hosting Online Courses	*140*
Getting Started Making and Selling Online Courses	*142*
Creating Your Course	*143*
Choosing Your Hosting Platform	*144*
Promoting Your Online Course	*145*
Chapter 16 Online Survey	**146**
Chapter 17 Network Marketing	**150**
Conclusion	**160**

Introduction

Are you struggling to make money? Do you feel like you are spending most of your time, yet you have nothing to show for it? If you have been trying to increase the number of passive income streams that you have but have been struggling to identify what streams to pursue, this book is perfect for you. There are eighteen ideas in here to help you begin building a passive income stream and earning a profit through these income streams in minimal timing. Each idea has been equipped with an explanation of the opportunity as well as everything you need to know to get started in that particular opportunity. While there is always more to learn, this will give you a running start in choosing your next opportunity and moving forward with it.

I encourage you to keep this book handy so that each time you master a passive income stream and mature it to the point of it producing you a consistent residual income, you have more ideas to explore in order to build another one. You can never have too many streams of residual income, so I encourage you to tap into as many resources as you possibly can and grow from there. The more you earn, the stronger your financial freedom and security will become—meaning that you will never have to worry about money again because you have so many sources coming in.

You may be wondering: if passive income is so important, why is it not more popular? Well, as you will learn, that is because passive income used to be something that was only afforded by those who had a significant amount of money to invest into the startup costs. Prior to the internet, generating a passive income stream took a large initial investment and a large network to make it work, which most people simply did not have access to. As a result, the average person did not have access to passive income, which meant that they had to have a hard work ethic and hopefully a strong savings plan in place to save enough for them to enjoy a few vacations and a retirement later in life.

Nowadays, getting involved in passive income is far more affordable and achievable for almost anyone— meaning, we all have fair access to generating multiple sources of passive income in our lives. This means that instead of having to save up for a retirement fund or a vacation and then no longer getting paid once you stop working for a period of time, you can continue getting paid no matter what you do. In fact, many people generate strong enough passive income streams, that they can retire young and still continue to collect checks through their passive income streams for the rest of their lives. These people are enjoying adventures, living their best lives, and inspiring the rest of us to begin generating as many passive income streams as we can so that we can also begin enjoying our lives more!

This book gives a comprehensive guide on the following:

- Understanding Passive Income
- Kindle-Publishing
- Amazon FBA
- Affiliate Marketing
- Dropshipping
- Retail arbitrage
- Cryptocurrency
- Stock Market
- Option Trading
- Dividend Investing
- Real estate

- Domain Flipping
- Shopify
- Virtual Assistant
- Online Courses
- Online Survey
- Network Marketing

I hope that in reading this guide that you will able to increase your understanding of how to generate large streams of passive income on your own and feel confident in doing so. From confidently investing in real estate to confidently investing through online trading, I hope that you will learn enough to get from point A to point B with less worry around how you can generate success along the way.

There is absolutely no limit to what you can achieve online, the more you explore, the more you discover the priceless opportunities that the digital space presents you. With the list of the various options that I have discussed with you in the book, no have absolutely no excuse to be broke again. Get started with one of the choices today and make the most out of it.

Remember, investing is never guaranteed no matter how conservative your investment portfolio is, so you should always be cautious around how you are investing and what you are investing in. This book is a great resource to help you get started, but I encourage you to really take your understanding and education even further when you decide which type of investment you want to get in on so that you feel confident in that investment.

Education truly is the best way to hedge yourself against risks as it cannot take the risk away completely but it can prevent you from making unnecessary mistakes or bad moves and losing your funds off of a simple mistake. You should never stop learning when you get started in investing as this is your opportunity to stay knowledgeable in the latest investing trends and strategies that you can leverage to improve your success.

Chapter 1 Understanding Passive Income

Passive income has become famous for many people who are tired of working 9 to 5 shifts. Different sources have defined the term differently. Besides, it leads to confusion about what this form of income is.

Some people confuse passive income for income with no effort. Although this may be true in later stages, it does not apply in the earlier step. This is why. Here is why.

The passive income might be achieved when you generate income without engaging directly in hard work.

That means that even if you don't work eight hours on your venture, revenue is still generated for you.

This does not assume, however, that you can bring in revenue without doing anything. During the earlier stage, you have to do the real job yourself.

So, you might ask, what is passive income?

Here's the stuff you ought to know.

The money you earn without spending much time is what you call passive income. For some, it is an investment; for others, it is royalty.

That means that you first invest time and money in a company.

If you are working and going, your income will be created even when you don't spend too much time on it. In other words, create a system, let it work for you, produce profits from the process, and find the way to freedom.

That's how you let money work for you rather than money.

What is passive revenue? It's the money you earn if you work hard right now and make it later.

One of the most popular ways to do that is to build a company, enforce the process, pay people to run the company, and sustain revenue.

Although some individuals acquire business from the beginning, others begin to grow smaller and later with higher incomes. When the company expands, you let the money work for you even as you sleep.

After defining what passive income is, it is also important to note what it IS NOT. For a more unobstructed view, here are some examples.

Sidelines producing side income are not equivalent to passive income. Let's claim that you keep a blog site and earn it. You cannot gain passive revenue without promoting any ads on the website through affiliate marketing.

On the other hand, wage increases are also not regarded as passive income. Although additional profits are produced at the same time, you still must operate for a particular duration. An uptick is just an increase in an employee's income. Consequently, passive income is not equal.

Since having established what may be passive income and what's not, you have a clearer picture of the path to financial independence. And may it assist you, like many others, along this highway.

There are two main income categories: active and passive

Passive Income

Passive income from businesses, leases, dividends, or other undertakings in which an individual is not actively engaged. Receives passive income through the royalties of this book. He used to write the book once. His publisher will print his book, and the bookstores will then market his book. He does not have to be involved in selling his book, but he still earns a regular income.

Active Income

percent Total profits in return for a person's services. It includes wages, tips, fees, and earnings from companies and jobs in which he/she is involved.

The money works for you because of passive income, rather than fighting for your money. A minority of people are surviving on the passive income, and almost no one is affluent.

Many people live on Passive Pay. They are expected to trade for money in their time. Most people work from eight to five. And many others have odd work to earn a fixed income. Most active income earners hardly have enough money to retire and have to work their whole lives. We are constrained and robbed of time by their work. We have no financial freedom and no freedom of time.

Their profit ends if they stop working.

Will you earn an active or a passive income?

Unless you want to be rich, you understand you still must gain a passive income.

Personal finance gurus are always speaking about how you must have enough passive income to outweigh your expenses to become financially free. That's good, but what's passive income, and how are you getting it?

In their purest form, profits can be categorized into 4 categories: income gained, investment income, passive income and leveraged income.

• As you probably figured, earned an income is a money that needs you to pay. Money is earned from your time and energy. Many people earn their living as an employee.

• Asset income is interest, capital gains and dividends resulting from the holding of inventories, mutual funds and bonds.

• Leveraged income was created by earning more money with bigger audiences. For example, a speaker in a conference can do as much to organize and give 20 people a speech as 1,000 people but can receive much more money from the larger group.

• Passive income is income that needs an initial investment and continues to pay for it, while the necessary participation dissipates. The first created effort a cash machine, which often brings money, even if the turnout is minimal.

• You could tell from above, earned income pays you only what you put in. In other words, it takes your time and your time. You can receive bonuses and promotions, but the sales are limited because only one of you is there.

On the other hand, with passive income, you can create multiple income streams, which will continue to generate money long after you have worked, when you continue to add more and more money sources, the passive income and asset flow increasing.

The Truth About Passive Income

If you're searching the internet for "passive income," you may find one or two examples, but most of them are websites that attempt to sell you on the day-of-day passive income. We agree it's frustrating. We don't know about you, but we do research before I leap in any chance, or before I take a trip. There are plenty of excellent opportunities. But let us talk about what passive income is and, most importantly, what it is not until you start to spend money.

The Webster describes passive income as "from, linked to, and in which the shareholder does not have immediate control over profits." Don't think the whole story tells that. The passive income is cash you regularly earn without much effort (not to mention that we didn't say "any job"). It's different from income earned because you don't get money for your time (like a job). But you can also have immediate control of your profits depending on the passive income source that you choose. But later I'm going to get to that.

Why would you like to earn passive income? Okay, this is the significant disparity between the wealthy and middle classes, as Robert Kiyosaki describes in his book Rich Dad Poor Dad. The wealthy invest their money in different streams of passive income. If your passive income exceeds your expenses, you are financially free. "Financially secure" means you don't have to work a day to pay your bills. And then you are "free" to do anything you want!

What Passive Income Isn't

What passive income does not mean until we ask you what passive income is, first let me remind you that it is not? Low income is not the same as "residual income." Residual income is cash that you regularly receive once you've finished your job. TV sitcoms are the best example. Some actors are getting "residuals." The actors are paid to shoot the show. Many performers are then paid every time the series repeats. Salespersons that sell services, products, and recycled items (such as insurance) will once sell the product and earn a fee from each sale by offering consumer renewals. Book and music publishing royalties are also available.

Some claim that multi-level marketing and network sales generate passive income for you. Guess what? Guess what? This is also residual.

If you have or are a small business, even if you make a lot of money, then this is NOT passive income. If you get a paycheck from your job, the money is earned. Nonetheless, there is a way to make this passive income-so stay tuned.

You know, we must claim that it can not be passive income to start your platform. Whether you sell a product (such as an eBook, a seminar, or other information) or a service, your website will continue to be promoted. You must do this irrespective of whether you offer your goods or can sell other products. Marketing your website is easy. It's not a job, though. And once the marketing efforts begin to go off, with little extra effort, you can make a lot of money. But this is residual, not active, in my novel.

What Passive Income IS

What Passive Revenue IS Massive Revenue is a lot? The first thing that comes to mind, and we agree that the most famous example is immobilization. If your investment property has a positive cash flow from a home, business property, or apartment, that is passive income. The passive income is also when you rent rooms in your home. You must set it up once, and then the income comes every month. Savings accounts, Bonds, and financial-market funds interest income is passive-the bank pays for keeping your money in those accounts. If you have a website that features banner ads and Google AdSense ads, it can also be considered passive.

When you invest in but do not run a company, your profits are called passive income, precisely what Webster meant when he wrote the concept.

What about the company? Okay, it depends on how you configure it. Rich people build companies and develop a system that the company follows. So, if the owner goes on vacation in Fiji for a month, the workers obey the plan, and the owner still gets the income. Of course, every business would start with a lot of work, but if you take the time to set up a company to generate reproducible results (just like a franchise), these profits will be passive. And any salary you receive from your business is considered "earned," but profit is considered "passive," according to the IRS. It is essential to work with an accountant and a lawyer to set up your business that will help you most financially.

What else would the passive income be termed? How about self-storage, parking garages, and dry cleaners! They all need some time to start, but once set up, and you get money back and forth.

Residual vs Passive Income

Rest and Passive Income Active and passive income are like relatives. Both are very similar, and most people regard them as synonyms. Nonetheless, what does it matter? Both are great ways of getting cash into your hands month by month without selling your time or independence. How could it get better?

Reality Check

Be wary of anyone who claims that passive income does NOT require work. Passive earnings mean no jobs! When you invest in a corporation, a stock, or an immovable property, you will have to do your research (called "due diligence"). The study is work! Work is work! You will also have to control your savings, track their progress, and adjust when necessary. This is work too! This is work too!

The real kicker is that research and administration is only a part-time effort. And this work can be done most of the time from almost anywhere, including on a beach in Fiji.

Don't forget about the FUN factor. I'm sure some of you read this, still enjoy their job (if you still have one). Some of you have a company of your own-and I congratulate you! But most of us work simply because we must feed our families and pay the bills. Looking at passive revenue streams and spending your time and money will produce many, many revenues. FUN is to look for and execute your passive income plans to fulfill your dreams. It's FUN every month, week, or even every day to get money. And checking and handling your money-if you have something to handle-is FUN.

Passive income is income, whether you work, sleep, or play. Passive income The American, Internal Revenue Service, determines profits from "trade or business activities in which you are not interested." Examples include:

- Rental income from real estate

- Profits from companies that do not require direct involvement or participation from the operator

- Royalties from book publishing or selling intellectual property

- Profits from internet advertising

- An insurance agent, for example, may gain a residual income when its customers renew insurance policies.

- However, the income goes away if the insurance agent leaves the company.

When you invest in a networking or multilevel marketing company in which you must continue to work to earn an income, that is not passive income either. If, if you want and still earn income, you can stop working together, that's passive income.

The big myth about passive income is that you're finished when you buy or build an asset for you. You may feel that you don't have to spend or manage more time on it.

The reality is that there are different degrees of "passive" employment, for example, but the property may be extremely time-consuming. Usually, there is an initial stabilization process when you buy a property, ranging from making repairs to locating and testing new tenants. Once the property is secured, you can sit and get rental checks for a while, but the occupant either leaves or the water heater fails, or a tree falls on your house, and you must spend time on the property once more.

This is not the same from a deposit certificate at bank where you receive it, and that is it. For example, when you know what you're doing, the actual profits for the rental property are much higher than the potential revenue on the deposit certificate.

Know how passive and residual income are unique, and how exactly "passive" an asset is. Why is passive income essential?

Imagine if you had no job, wife, family, state, or anyone else to rely on for money. This form of income can provide you with.

Across various traditional models of financial planning, you are encouraged to find out how much cash you need to withdraw. You spend that money on retirement. This strategy has some serious shortcomings. What if you live longer than you expected and save your cash first? Secondly, what if you would like to leave it after putting so much energy into saving that money rather than spending it?

PI > E If your Passive Income (PI) is more significant than your expenditures (E), you are entirely free to choose how to use your time because your resources continue to pay for your lifestyle, whether you are working or not.

The reality is you don't need to be free of debt to be financially independent, pay off your home, make a ton of money, or become a millionaire. You need more revenue than expenditure.

It's that easy.

You may choose to stay out of joy and freedom instead of obligation or debt. Passive income allows you to have more choices.

What if something awful happened and you couldn't work anymore, on a more serious note? How are you going to pay your bills? You also have more peace of mind when you have enough passive income.

This equation has two components. You can increase your passive income to become financially independent quicker, and you can also explore how to reduce your expenses.

So how are you getting more passive revenue?

Two main types of passive income exist. Passive investment income is the first type. You need funds to invest in these income instruments to earn passive investment profits. If you have funds to invest, you need to rely on analysis and due diligence to decide which of the passive tools best suit your situation and perception for risk.

The second type comes from creating a small or no money own income vehicle. For example, you may be opening a website that produces ad revenue or joining a network marketing agency that allows you to continue receiving income when you are no longer active. Or you may start your own business or become an affiliate of another corporation.

If you already have money to invest, you can probably generate profits faster than anyone who doesn't. If you don't have any money to invest, you should give time, energy, expertise, capital, imagination, or all.

Sources of Passive Income

It is difficult to find income sources today. There is a widening gap between rich and poor. Others claim you always have the income to survive when you work hard. But what are you going to do if it's challenging to find a job? Even the rich find it difficult to keep their income. Nonetheless, for those who know where to find sources of passive income, this is less of a concern.

Let us, then, first describe passive income. Passive income is a form of investment income. Two types of income are available-active and passive. We gain a successful income from our jobs. Salaries, fees, and service charges are useful income sources. What are passive income sources? Income sources have various forms. Some familiar causes include earned interests, dividends, sales, land, equipment, cash, and rent.

Dividend

The dividend is received from a company's net income. It is a way of sharing income and is more prevalent in the stock market. If more than one person owns a company, the income is divided according to the assets of each shareholder. This owner is called shareholder, and a dividend is referred to as a profit. Money or stock can be the dividend. It is a cash bonus when bank checks pay the gain in cash. And it is a portfolio dividend if allocated as stocks or bonds. Dividend is also an attractive source of passive income, especially during the growing period. Not all firms are paying stable dividends. It is important to remember that the selection of stocks determines your future revenue. If the chosen business has shown higher dividends, it will be highly likely to continue. Income stocks are named some firms that consistently make higher dividends. Revenue stocks may not be large corporations.

Nevertheless, even some large companies fail to make regular dividends because of their high operating costs. Not all stocks are, therefore, sure that they are one of the sources of passive revenue.

The "capital inventory," which relies on a pleasant industry environment, is one of the many sources of income on the stock market. For example, any IT company can be a candidate as a source of passive income if the IT sector is beautiful. This suggests that choosing such businesses is safer than selecting a large company that has been facing economic turmoil in the market. A business from a strong sector is, therefore, a good source of passive income in the stock market.

Interest Earned

The interest earned is also popular as a source of passive income. Our money collects an interest rate if we deposit our money in a bank. What is the rate of interest? The interest rate is the amount paid when we borrow money, and when we borrow, it is received. While we're not a creditor, we can make it because the money we deposited in the bank adds to the amount that the lender has loaned to the lenders. Before we see our deposits as sources of income, there is a requirement.

We may consider our investments as a source of passive income. It occurs only after the market rate is high, and our investment is considerable. Time deposits and bank bonds are examples of liabilities. A savings account can also be one. Banks vary in interest rates from each other. To obtain attractive income from the banks, we should choose the right bank and deposit when the interest rate is high.

Rent and Lease

Lease and Rent Passive income sources are multiple and dynamic. However, lease and rent were the simplest. Without a doubt, everybody knows that our income is proven to give us a stable source of income by making our property leased or rented. If you have a new house and a lot or an apartment unit, you only need someone to take place. Your sources of passive income here are not your land, but a stable tenant who can reliably pay the rent and stay longer. The only factor here is your tenant's profile. If the property is a commercial estate, you may have to rent a bar, a gas station, or a warehouse to those businessmen. Your tenant's profile here is more reliable than the household. Commercial lot tenants are certainly going to stay longer. This can be your company because this kind of investment is not liquid. It is an investment in the long term. Nevertheless, many of us will consider this as one of the most reliable sources of income.

Nonetheless, investment in transport services is hardly regarded as one of the potential sources. The threat here is high. But if you are just an average person who owns one or two units of a taxi, lease them out if you are spending a little in the depreciation of your car.

Sales

Sales Business Buy-and-sell may be sources of revenue depending on the services or goods you sold. That your company, the more passive your income is. It's advertising and a good source of adequate income when we exchange smaller things. But if cars, houses and lots, stocks and bonds are what they buy and sell, they are significant sources of passive revenue.

Land

The land is the most significant source of revenue. It doesn't need to be rented out. It has been the most secure source of income since time immemorial. In the past, fertile soil can grow without human intervention crops, trees, plants, and grains. Also, livestock and poultry were fertile land commodities. All these items that land can generate are passive income sources. Until now, but with little interference, these conditions are still valid.

Equipment

Equipment is one of the origins of passive income in the country. Rice Mill is the most common equipment on the farm. Farmers are lining their rice sacks to a milling station during the harvest season. An owner of a rice mill will get a certain amount per bag. After the harvest season, the rice mill owners ' cash flow is much healthier than farmers '. Rice mills are hardly needed in the post-harvest season. Some other crops and grains are, however, required by other equipment. Shelling devices and graders are at the front for peanuts. Dryers, farm tractors, and grinders are different forms of machinery on the farm.

Equipment is one of the best sources of passive income, even in the region. Heavy construction equipment can be leased to contractors and builders. If you are an average person, you can buy a dealer. A dealer is being leased. You are gaining from your sold products. It's a passive income, though, because it's your computer that works for you. The printing press is the most common and most heavily rented equipment in the region. This is a company and an investment at the same time.

Now we see that there are a lot of income sources. It's wise to invest it in something that gives us income to spend, rather than spending so much money on consumption. We should save our active income, and our passive income is the one we can invest in. Our wise choices are, therefore, also sources of passive income.

Passive Income Opportunity in Stock Trading

Chances come in many ways. Some people say it only knocks once. Others say it lingers. The reality isn't a big deal. It's how you get the chance. Many people will agree that the best opportunity they can have is an income opportunity. That's why everyone searches for it. Yet, it could hardly be noticed by some. It does not necessarily involve much effort to get the chance. The lion is a good analogy. Following ten tries, lions get their prey. They will have used all their food by the time they kill their prey. Your diet is just enough to replace your lost energy, and that energy is just enough to take another day off. On the other side, crocodiles float on the water, wait for their prey, and never let it go. They'll be full and not hungry for a long time after their meal before finding another live victim. The latter is the best example of how to get a shot. And this example is like a passive income incentive in terms of income opportunities.

A careful examination of the economic situation impacting the danger-reward ratio of a specific investment method can be used to consider passive income opportunities. When you invest in the stock market, the right opportunity is if the price of a business you are willing to purchase is at its lowest level. In this case, it is cheap, and the stock valuation value is high. This is another forum for passive income. In the stock market, we benefit from a company's dividends and at the same time, from its appraisal. Taking use of price fluctuations provides some incentives for passive income. Ideally, they buy shares at low prices and sell them at low prices. This also applies to nearly all trading instruments. When a clear and strong pattern emerges, a passive income potential becomes apparent. To make the correct entry, we should understand why these changes take place so that we can monitor the course of the market. The price action of one instrument is essential to know to determine the capacity and limit of a passive income opportunity, and this is determined by the changing market conditions guided by numerous different factors, from which we also have to learn profoundly.

Traders use two methods for assessing a passive income asset, which is known as essential and technical analysis. Fundamental analysis is a tool for analyzing current economic factors affecting consumer behavior. When the financial situation is excellent, it promises a positive investment growth. Traders are, therefore, ready to buy attractive devices. And by doing this, they force the other market players to raise their prices. But if the economic situation is worse, concerns are triggered, and this is known as an aversion to risk. The latter is referred to as risk appetite.

We can calculate economic strength and weakness using periodic economic indicators. GDP is one of the most famous symbols of the economy. When the GDP number is higher than expected, the economy is stable and investment friendly. The unemployment rate is another important indicator. Consumers are reluctant to spend when the unemployment rate is higher. Industries are struggling. And so, it's a bad investment moment. This is just one example of the importance of each information for traders to make a sound decision. Good economic indicators also provide investors and traders with a passive income incentive.

This economic news can affect the feelings of the consumer. Nonetheless, rumors often make traders respond more than the news. Most traders, therefore, buy stories and sell the news. This is also another area for passive income. How does it work? How does it work? For example, if a company were to launch a highly competitive product, investors would purchase the business a lot earlier. The value of the company would, therefore, also be lower. And if the news isn't real, early purchasers will sell and benefit. Knowledge thus provides us with a passive income incentive.

The use of technical analysis is another approach that traders use to define a passive revenue opportunity. Technical analysis provides traders with historical graph data. The graph may display trends that allow traders to follow the market trend. It also sends a signal that the value of a trading instrument exceeds a certain point where each time a reversal happens. A passive income potential starts when the graph shows a clear trend right after a setback. Experts in this field have various instruments for disclosing a passive income chance. Price is shifting within a trading range here. If the array is disrupted, however, it means a significantly stronger pattern. This is considered a "break-out." A breakthrough event is an excellent opportunity for passive income. The purchasing of an explosion has proven lucrative.

Regardless of whether fundamental or technological approaches are employed, there is always a passive income chance.

There are still other ways of finding passive income, such as new trading instruments. These include the IPO, public bond sales, and any new investment instrument issue. In summary, because it is a new problem, the price is lowest, and there is no way to go up.

The initial public offer (IPO) is a new share problem for the growth of a business. Companies need not borrow money from banks to expand their operations. Instead, they would search for investors to collect their funds to finance the expansion process. The new problem has still not been sold on the stock market. When a company executes the IPO, investment banks buy the new stock issue. Afterward, investment banks will pay for the company. Then the current item purchased by the investment bank will be sold on the stock exchange trading floor. This form of sale in the store is known as an IPO. Why many investors want to purchase an IPO is that most of the businesses that issue an IPO are expanding. When it develops, a company grows, and potential growth is active in the near term. The IPO of a growing company is also sold at the lowest price. The market path is therefore set to a bullish pattern. Those shares will be traded after the initial public offering. Such dividends will become secondary stocks if they are passed from one investor to another. IPO is an excellent example of passive income. Rumors about an IPO increase risk appetite on the stock market. During the economic slowdown, IPO is hardly seen except for the sector to which it belongs. A passive income opportunity begins when the economy is continuously growing, especially if the company that issues the IPO is the primary beneficiary.

Fusion and acquisition also create a passive income incentive because investing in the giant is always enticing.

We saw many possibilities for seeking passive income. If you are still not determined to try one on your own, people who specialize in trading these instruments also have a passive income opportunity. You can ask fund managers for advice. Many high-net-worth people invest in these traders ' proven talents. You can study the way they do about passive income opportunities if you choose to do so. It is also wise to invest in people who already benefit from passive income.

Chapter 2 Kindle-Publishing

Outsourcing is one of the ways many of the books are getting published through Kindle. There are writers who are not confident enough to publish under their own name, do not have the savings to publish and market their books, or simply want to focus on the writing versus the marketing of books.

Writers are hired to ghostwrite various topics. They may have a special niche that they deal with or a vast knowledge that allows the writer to discuss more than one topic. Savvy writers choose concepts they consider themselves experts in, as a way to offer validity of the products they are hired to create.

A publishing company may contact a pool of writers directly. They will create a writer's persona and have the writer create the product based on an outline or a title heading. The writer will get a flat rate with no potential to earn royalties from the book sales.

The publishing company or person is the one that receives the royalties. Sometimes there is a middle person who gets work from the publisher, passes it on to their pool of writers, and makes passive income from simply getting the completed book back to the publishing company.

Kindle allows anyone to publish a book. Quality is not always the best because Kindle doesn't check, with as much scrutiny, as other eBook publishing sites. There are certain things that Kindle looks for, such as sensitive topics like inappropriate photos, foul language, broken grammar, etc. Other than that, nearly anything can be published.

All you have to do is set up an account with Amazon, in their KDP department. It is free to set up a publishing account. When you set up the account, you gain access to free tutorials on how to publish, the template you need to use, and the various options for making money from the published book. You also gain access to emails that help you see what is hot or trending right now. Furthermore, Amazon will help you get book covers from a pool of template images. When the book is published, you can choose to make it exclusive to Kindle, meaning you will not publish the book elsewhere. This helps you gain a higher royalty amount. You can also opt to sell it in multiple locations to garner more customers and make less on the royalties at these various publishing locations.

How to Make It Work for You

As you can imagine, there are certain ways for you to make more money from Kindle publishing than others.

- You can write the book.
- Upload it.
- Market it.

Your other option is to pay a flat rate to a writer, so they get the time-consuming work of researching the topic, writing the book, and editing it. Then, you reap the rewards of uploading it and marketing it.

The money is truly in where and how you market the book.

Marketing with Kindle Publishing

One of the great things about Kindle is that they do market your book for you. However, you have hundreds of books being written each month, on similar topics, so even Kindle cannot market each book with the same success.

You want to take advantage of what they will do to market the book, but also have your own methods.

- Use email lists
- Set up affiliate marketing sites
- Create a blog
- Use social media

The email list option that will be discussed later will help you garner people that are more interested in the books you are selling. Of course, they have to buy or read your book first.

The key here is to offer your book for a limited time at a "free to read" price. This is where you put it in the Kindle Unlimited option for free. Someone sees the topic because they are interested in it, reads it, and then opts-in to read more books when you publish a new one.

When you have readers through Kindle Unlimited or offer the book for free for a short time, you want these individuals to leave a review. You should ask in the email or at the end of the book for a review. You don't have to be obvious about it but ask the person to let others know how much the reader appreciated the content.

Obviously, you want more positive reviews than negative reviews. If there are issues with your book, a rewrite to correct them should be made, so that you are selling a quality product.

Using affiliate marketing sites, you can create multiple online websites selling the books or at least products related to the books' topics. For example, if you grow pineapples, set up a website to sell pineapples. Post that you have books on how to grow, care, and repot pineapples available on Kindle. An interested customer will click through to your Amazon site and purchase the book. You have just made a sale to them for a pineapple plant and a book. Now you have two sources making you passive income.

You will always need a blog. When a new book comes out, you will use a press release or a book review by a customer to post on the blog. Readers flock to the blog, follow the link, and buy the book. The link they follow is, of course, an ad for that book.

Social media outlets are also ways to let people know that you have a book available to read. You can use your friends, family (with permission, of course), as well as anyone who stops by your social media websites.

Ratings

Profitability - Most of the hard work in Kindle publishing is over once you have finished your book. After submitting and publishing your book, the majority of the proceeds are passive in nature.

Perspective in the future - To scale your publishing business, you can either write more books or create bundles using your existing books. The more books you have the more royalties you can earn from sales.

Difficulty - As long as your manuscript is up to par with Amazon's standards, there are very little barriers along the way. You can have your book published by Amazon in a few days.

Budget for starting – As low as $100.

Chapter 3 Amazon FBA

The program's business model is very similar to that of dropshipping. If you are familiar with dropshipping or if you have experience with it, you will find it easy to understand Amazon FBA's business model. This opportunity can be very lucrative if you can think of a product that has very little competition within the Amazon network. The whole process can be simplified in the following steps:

1. You apply for the Amazon FBA program.
2. If you are accepted, you ship your products to one of their distribution centers. The company refers to these distribution centers as fulfillment centers.
3. You list your products for sale in Amazon.
4. If someone buys your product, Amazon ships the product to the customer.

Looking at the business model of the program, it's easy to recognize obvious benefits. For one, Amazon handles the sales and shipping process. The company receives the orders, process them, and ship the products. They are literally running the business for you. Your main responsibility is to keep on sending more of your products to Amazon's fulfillment centers before these run out of stock.

Earlier, we've mentioned how the business model is very similar to dropshipping. This is because you can turn it into a real dropshipping business. You can enter into a contract with a manufacturer or a supplier who makes the products then ship these on your behalf to Amazon's fulfilment centers. In this setup, your role is to make sure that the supplier keeps making and shipping the products. You can also choose to have the supplier send the products to you so that you will be the one shipping the products to Amazon. This is a good idea if you want to make sure that the products you are selling are of the highest quality possible.

Ratings Based on Our Criteria

1. Simplicity:

Starting a business with Amazon FBA can be very complicated because there are a lot of hoops you have to go through. You have to apply with the program. You need to make sure that the products pass certain standards (e.g. packaging and safety requirements) etc. And you have to be communicating with your manufacturer/supplier, inspectors etc. to make sure products are manufactured to specification. If they happen to be in China, the language barrier and time zone difference could present challenges.

6/10

2. Passivity:

Managing an Amazon FBA business can take a lot of your time and resources. Some of your time will be spent communicating with your suppliers, optimizing your listings, running promotions/giveaways, Optimizing your Amazon sponsored ads etc. However, passivity can be improved by outsourcing some of these tasks to virtual assistants who will take care of them for you. Virtual assistants can be hired from fiverr.com or upwork.com.

6/10

3.   Scalability:

It's easy to scale your Amazon FBA business. Once you are accepted into the program and you have successfully launched your first product and familiarized yourself with the process, scaling is as simple as adding more products to your inventory or expanding your product offerings (i.e. offering your customers complementary products as part of a bundle).

9/10

4.   Competitiveness:

Expect a lot of other merchants selling similar products as you. You might even be getting your products from the same suppliers. Furthermore, it's not unusual to compete directly with suppliers from China.

4/10

Tips for Success

- Do your research before you jump into the bandwagon. As I've mentioned earlier, competition within Amazon is fierce. So what you need to do is research for products that have good demand but little competition. A good market research software for this is Jungle Scout or Viral Launch

- Watch and observe your most successful competitors. What are they doing? What tools are they using? What marketing strategies are they implementing? Learn about these and maybe apply them on your own business.

- Encourage your customers to leave reviews. The more reviews you get on Amazon, the greater the social proof and likelihood of it selling. However, do not offer incentives in exchange for review as this is against Amazon's terms of service.

- Optimize your product listings with the right keywords and descriptions. A good keyword research tool to consider is Merchant Words

- Use high-quality photos of your products. Ugly and unprofessional product photos can easily turn off customers.

- Only deal with reliable manufacturers and suppliers. If they screw up, then your business is equally screwed.

- Always check with Amazon to ensure that your products are in stock. Running out of stock can negatively affect your product rankings and once lost its difficult to regain.

- Personalize/brand your products to make them stand out from the others. This is important if you are getting your products from a supplier who is probably sending the same products to other merchants.

- Offer discounts and incentives to those who are buying in bulk. This is a great way to build loyalty among your customers.

- Always follow the rules, regulations, and standards as set forth by Amazon. Amazon can easily terminate your account if you break a rule or two.

FAQs

- What are the requirements in joining Amazon FBA?

- You are going to need the following: email address, standard mailing address, phone number, social security number, tax identification number, credit or debit card, bank account, and bank routing number.

- What are the costs of using Amazon FBA?

- When using FBA, you should expect to be paying for three specific types of fees: storage fees, fulfilment fees, and inventory placement fees. These are not fixed fees. They depend on the types of products you are sending them for storage. They will inform you about the amount of fees you are going to pay after finalizing your shipments.

- **How do I get products ready for Amazon FBA?**

- Every product you have must be individually packaged, properly labelled, and ready to be sold. You should also strictly follow the company's product stickering requirements.

- **Can I sell products overseas through Amazon FBA?**

- Yes, you absolutely can. Amazon is flexible when it comes to importing or exporting your products. However, you should keep in mind that selling your products overseas has additional fees, requirements, and other complications. Make sure that you take this into account and look into your financials to see if it's worth it to offer your products to overseas customers.

- How do I ship my products to any of Amazon's fulfilment centers?

- The full procedure is detailed in Amazon FBA's help section. You have to log into your Amazon FBA account, go to Manage Inventory and choose the Send and Replenish Inventory option. You have to completely and properly label your products before you ship them to Amazon's fulfilment centers. Improperly packaged products will cause a lot of problems which can be very costly on your part.

- What kind of products can I sell through Amazon FBA?

- Amazon FBA has a long list of restricted products so I highly suggest that you check it out. Here's the list of products that you can't sell on Amazon FBA as an independent seller:

- Alcohol
- Warranties, service plans, contracts and guarantees
- Tobacco and tobacco-related products
- Throwable personal flotation devices
- Surveillance equipment

- Subscriptions and periodicals
- String lights
- Stolen property and lock picking devices
- Squishy toys
- Sex and sensuality products
- Recycled electronics
- Recalled products
- FBA prohibited products exceptions
- Postage meters and stamps
- Plants, seeds, and other plant products
- Pesticides
- Personal electronic mobility devices or PEMs
- Organic products
- Offensive and controversial materials
- Medical devices and accessories
- Lighting products
- Laser products
- Jewelry and precious gems
- Invisible ink pens
- Infant sleep positioners
- Infant car seats
- Human parts and burial artefacts
- Hazardous and dangerous items
- Gambling and lottery products

- Chilled and frozen foods
- Food and beverages
- Fire and smoke masks
- Fire and other safety products
- Fidget spinners
- Export controls
- Explosives, weapons, and related items
- Electronics
- Eclipse glasses and filters for solar viewing
- Drugs and drug paraphernalia
- Dietary supplements
- Currency, coins, cash equivalents, and gift cards
- Cosmetics and skin and hair care
- Batteries and chargers
- Automotive and powersports
- Art home décor
- Fine art
- Animals and animal products
- Amazon devices: Fair Use and Compatibility Guidelines
- Amazon Device Accessories

- How safe are my products when I ship them to Amazon?

- There is always the possibility that your products can get lost during transit and storage. However, these problems are rare. As to security, Amazon has a payment fraud protection system that protects you from fraudulent orders and transactions.

- How much does it cost to sell on Amazon?

- Amazon offers two types of plans. The Professional Selling Plan costs $39.99 a month plus per item selling fees. The Individual Selling Plan is for sellers who only sells 40 items or less a month. This plan doesn't have a monthly fee. Instead, you pay a $0.99 fee for every item you sell.

- Who handles customer support on my Amazon FBA products?

- Customer support is the responsibility of Amazon. This is one of the biggest advantages of the Amazon FBA program. Once you shipped your products to their fulfilment centers, the company will handle the rest.

They will manage customer inquiries, refunds, and returns. It's worth mentioning here that Amazon's customer support is available 24 hours a day, seven days a week.

- Where can I get products to sell on Amazon FBA?

- There are several avenues that you can explore here. One, you can create your own products. Two, you can enter a deal with a supplier who provides you with products which you then label and package as your own. Three, you can explore retail arbitrage. That is you purchase products from other stores in bulk then sell them for a profit on Amazon. And four, you can consider private labelling or white labelling.

Myth Busters About Amazon FBA

- That it's very hard to sell products on Amazon. Yes, the system seems complicated but it's actually easy once you get the hang of it.
- That you can't be successful selling on Amazon because of the immense competition. Sure, the competition is tough but the market is also growing. In short, Amazon is still a very profitable side business.
- That you can just list your product and it will start selling like hotcakes. If you are to achieve success on Amazon, you don't just list a product, you have to market it like crazy.
- That you need your own website to sell on Amazon. Amazon itself serves as your online store. List your product and the company does the rest.
- That you need to invest a lot of money into Amazon. You can start a business on Amazon with just a few hundred dollars. In short, it's not that expensive.

- That inventory management is a pain in the head. Yes, it can be confusing at first but just like everything else, you will get used to it.
- That you need to give a lot of discounts to attract customers. Offering discounts surely helps but you don't have to if you are confident about the demand for your products.
- That Amazon doesn't care about you. The fact that the company welcomes independent sellers tells a very different story.
- That Amazon is losing its influence. This myth is perpetrated by competitors who want to steal sellers from Amazon and bring them into their own platforms.
- That you can get rich quick on Amazon. Don't entertain such an exaggerated idea. Of course, it's possible but you should be realistic with your goals.

Chapter 4 Affiliate Marketing

Affiliate marketing is one of the most popular passive income streams for people who are just getting into building an income in the online world. If you have ever scrolled on Instagram or Facebook and saw someone sharing an image of themselves using a product with a link to purchase the product, you have seen affiliate marketing in action. This particular marketing trend has grown massively in recent years because businesses have discovered that it is one of the leading opportunities to leverage social marketing without having to incur such a large marketing budget.

Benefits of Affiliate Marketing

Affiliate marketing is one of the easiest ways to leverage your personal brand. Whether you have already begun building your personal brand or if you are looking to get started specifically for the purpose of affiliate marketing, getting started is simple and making a profit is almost effortless. As long as you are willing to put in the time to build an audience and develop your following, you are going to have the capacity to earn an income through affiliate marketing.

Another massive benefit to affiliate marketing is if you are running a personal business in any industry, affiliate marketing is always a great way to boost your income. For example, if you are a personal trainer you could become an affiliate marketer for workout gear or protein powder companies, or if you are a chef you could become an affiliate marketer for various food prep companies or meal services. The opportunities to add affiliate marketing into almost any existing brand are endless, making it a versatile, effective, and easy to access market for virtually anyone to get into.

How You Earn Money This Way

Earning money through affiliate marketing is simple: you use products and share them with your audience and any time your audience purchases products from a company through you, you are paid for that purchase. Often, your followers will purchase either through a custom link or using a unique discount code that shows the company that it was your follower who made the purchase. As long as your customers use that promo code or link, you will be paid a certain commission depending on what the affiliate marketing agreement stated in the beginning.

Getting Started With Affiliate Marketing

Getting started in affiliate marketing only requires two things: a niche, and an audience. Once you have these two things in place, you can begin approaching companies or affiliate marketing programs to get connected with potential brands who want to leverage your brand power to market to your shared audience. The following steps will help you get started with affiliate marketing in the simplest manner possible.

Choosing Your Niche

The first thing that you need to do before getting into affiliate marketing is choosing your niche. If you already have a brand in place, then you have probably already put effort into building a specific niche and targeting a certain audience. If you have a large social media following but you have never really identified yourself as being a person with a particular niche, getting started narrowing down your niche and getting your audience used to your new focus is important. This way, you are going to have an audience filled with qualified leads who are more likely to purchase products through your unique links or codes.

If you are unsure as to what niche to target, consider what your interests are and what companies you would be most interested in working with. Then, consider who their target audience would be and who they are trying to reach through their marketing campaigns. You can easily learn more about this by looking at the websites and social media profiles of the brands you want to enter an affiliate deal with. Once you have identified their niche and their combined target audience, you can foster the same niche and target audience for yourself. This way, you are building the exact audience that your desired partners want to be reaching, making you an asset to their businesses when it comes to marketing.

Building Your Audience

If you do not already have an audience, you are going to want to start building one. This part can be somewhat time-consuming, but this is where your foundation for affiliate marketing will be built from. Once your foundation is strong, maintaining your audience and building your sales will be significantly easier for you to do, making it easier for you to be able to turn this into a truly passive income stream.

Building your audience essentially requires you to determine where your audience spends their time online and then building your presence there. You will need to invest some time in learning the unique marketing strategies used on each unique platform so that you can reach your audience effectively. You want to avoid using a "one size fits all" approach, as this will result in you experiencing a lot of failure in your marketing strategies across many platforms. If you are brand new to marketing, consider starting on just one platform and then building out from there so that you can spend more time really mastering that particular platform first. Once you have mastered it, you can move on to your next platform, and so on and so forth until you are successfully balancing every platform that your audience spends their time on. Typically, this is only one or two, maybe three different platforms so it should be quite simple, and you can easily use third-party programs like Hootsuite or Buffer to prepare your posts for various platforms in advance. That way, you do not have to spend so much time marketing across various platforms.

Aside from mastering each unique platform, you will need to foster three important marketing elements:

authenticity, consistency, and sincerity. When you build your brand using an authentic approach and you remain consistent in doing so, people begin to see who you truly are and develop a relationship with your brand. As a result, they are more likely to remember you amongst everyone else and keep their eyes turned towards you and your page, meaning that you have a higher chance of succeeding at affiliate marketing. Furthermore, when you remain sincere and seek to build genuine relationships with your followers, they trust you more which makes them more likely to purchase from your links.

Finding Affiliate Programs

The last step in building your successful passive income stream through affiliate marketing is finding affiliate programs! You can easily find programs early on through platforms like Clickbank, or you can approach the companies that you are most interested in working with using a request to become an affiliate for them. If you do choose to approach a company, make sure that you are prepared to sell your services to them by helping them see how valuable your marketing is and how aligned your audience is with theirs. You are going to need to show them how you can be an asset to their business and why they should consider paying you a commission for marketing their products. Always stay professional in your conversations as well to avoid having brands see you as unprofessional, as they will not only be considering your platform and your marketing abilities but also your persona. Brands want to make sure that you are going to portray them through a positive image and that your message and personality will accurately reflect them and their brands, too.

As an affiliate marketer, you will need to continually seek out new deals until you become large enough that companies begin seeking you out. Aside from reaching out to new companies and posting to keep your audience engaged and to show them your links, however, there is not a lot to affiliate marketing! Most of your money will be made when you are off living your life and other people are coming across your content online while they scroll through their newsfeeds.

Chapter 5 Dropshipping

It's a way of selling items to your customers without keeping your stock. You just let the supplier know when an order has been placed, and they will ship to the customer directly.

It can be very efficient and easy to do. That's the way many eBay Power Sellers work. However, it can be challenging to find the right suppliers, which is why most people use a wholesale drop shipping directory to help them find quality and reliable suppliers.

To create massive income streams on the internet, most individuals use drop shipping. You've probably heard of people living from eBay making their full-time living. Perhaps, many people are checking out local garage sales, picking up some things, and selling them online. But most people who make big money don't see the goods they're making. They don't even pay in advance for them.

Drop shipping is becoming an effortless way for people to benefit from home without any cash start-up in their spare time.

The definition is easy to grasp, but when you need to find a supplier, the hard part comes. This move is crucial and will decide how much money you're making. You need to find a supplier that sells your product at a price you can make a profit. It may seem like an impossible task if you don't know where to look.

Do what most people do-look for distributors in dropship and retail directories if you want to save yourself time and headache. Such lists compile suppliers in one location, actual and sometimes pre-screened (depending on the list), so users can easily browse through to find those that meet their needs.

You will be able to compare rates with your membership, read reviews, and see the experiences of other people to ensure the supplier is legit. Online scams have caught a lot of people don't let that happen to you.

Additionally, many of these databases come with teaching materials and private forums, so you know you're not going to be alone if you ever need help or have any questions.

How to Start Drop shipping Successfully

Over the past few decades, the entire spectrum of doing business has experienced a lot of transition. Dropship services are one of the latest online business ideas. This online business requires a process in which producers or distributors supply the products directly to the dropship business customers without having to buy or store the goods in advance. The best part of the deal is that no hard work, such as inventing, designing, purchasing, and producing the product, checking the demand, presenting the product on the internet, making the website appealing or selling the product, has to be done by the business owner or reseller.

The business owner of drop ship services has to list the products on eBay and get orders for the products using the specifications and graphics of their own or the distributor firm. The reseller provides information on the names and addresses of the customers and other specifics of the order when the orders are issued so that the manufacturer can deliver the goods to the customer. The client also receives the fee.

The market of dropship service may yield rich returns for the small businessman, but the most significant drop shipping guide is that it is necessary to take care of the company and customers and ensure that any purchaser's concerns about poor product performance or delays between receiving payments and delivering goods are promptly tendentious. Any negligence in providing the necessary after-sales services and dealing with complaints that tarnish the company's image and lead to loss of revenue and potential orders. It is vital to choose a reliable supplier to find an answer to how to dropship and how to begin a drop shipping company. False selection can result in disastrous results. Before starting this type of business, follow the following steps.

1) Choose Recommended Suppliers: The very first step to begin the business of dropship services is that suppliers should be selected very carefully. Select other people's suggested suppliers. Lists of drop shipping companies can be downloaded free or charged on Internet directory pages. Most have accurate information, while unscrupulous vendors may operate others, so avoid such specific recommendations.

2) Check the contact information: once a choice has been made based on credible advice and after ensuring that the supplier provides the range of products that the client wants to work with, check the contact details

issued by the supplier. Relevant contact information such as telephone number, email address, and mailing address should be available on the website of the supplier. Remove any company that has inaccurate or no contact information at all. Make sure the phone is answered and see how long it takes the manufacturer to respond to emails, which may be useful later if you have a reason to contact them with a question.

3) Check the terms and conditions of the supplier: because there may be conflicts with the supplier regarding faulty products or non-delivered goods, the terms and conditions of the supplier should be appropriately specified and understood by the reseller. Realize that the company as a reseller's obligations are different from the duties the distributor will have towards the reseller.

4) Unreasonable subscription charges: the dropship services company as a reseller must pay reseller registration fees and, in some cases, continuing subscription fees for the right of access to the supplier's catalog. Access is usually allowed before registration for a limited time. Test to see if it pays recurring subscription fees before registering with any supplier.

Fine printing should also be carefully checked for any clauses between the lines.

5) Beware of intermediaries Disguised as suppliers: check that the prospective supplier has enough inventory of the goods and that they are not intermediaries posing as suppliers. Such intermediaries place orders with the actual supplier, and there may be extended delays when they obtain warrants from the reseller. Such delays can result in losses to the consumer and, subsequent loss to reseller due to the repayment of the fee.

6) Payment methods: find out how the manufacturer wants payments to be collected as the most convenient method would be the same as the customer's payment method. This will save money and costs. It is also best to avoid having paying for Telegraph Transfer or Wire Transfer because if there is no consumer service, the risk is higher.

7) Look out for companies selling fake goods: avoid such sites offering branded goods such as designer clothing or electrical goods at incredibly low prices when selecting a manufacturer. These low-priced, so-called designer products are likely to be counterfeit unless the

manufacturer is renowned and trustworthy, and the goods are purchased from a close-out, or if the goods are refurbished or returns from Grade A. If the dealer sells fake products, he may be charged with selling counterfeit goods.

8) Search for Online Reviews: after a few suppliers have been shortlisted, it would be useful to check for reviews and suggestions from other dropship resellers on the Internet forums. Although it may be hard to find any good comments as resellers do not want others to know about their lucrative origin, bad reviews will certainly help make the right decision.

9) Search for artists and craftsmen: a unique way to do dropship services business is to team up with artists and artisans for their creative goods. Generally, these creative people lack knowledge of advertising. Visits to local trade fairs will offer unlimited opportunities to buy amazing original products at incredibly low prices compared to eBay prices. Such products do not need to be purchased by the dropship company, but an agreement could be made to work on commission. We will probably be happy when a sale is made to the buyer of the dropship business to take his fee and deliver the goods.

Chapter 6 Retail arbitrage

If you are interested in selling physical items online and don't want the hassle of opening your own online store, then retail arbitrage might be for you. Originally an exclusive to those who traded in the foreign exchange currency market, arbitrage is simply the idea of purchasing a commodity at one price and then selling it elsewhere for a higher price. The rise of online marketplaces means that anyone can participate in retail arbitrage, as long as they are able to purchase items at a price that means they can be resold elsewhere for a profit.

Starting out: The biggest asset when it comes to retail arbitrage is a good nose for a great bargain. Your two biggest assets in this quest are going to be the Amazon Price check app and the eBay seller's application as these two sites are typically going to be the best place to go to sell your items for a profit. Both of these applications will help you determine the baseline price an item is selling for so you can decide if the price you are considering purchasing it at is worth the trouble.

In addition to these free applications, consider the Profit Bandit application. While it has a $10 upfront cost, it provides you with a wide variety of information that the free apps lack. Specifically, it will tell you how the current price of an item stacks up to the price of that item overall and also if the product is being sold by Amazon directly or if it violates their code of conduct and why. It will inform you the amount of profit you stand to make off of an item based on the amount you are paying, the amount you will sell it for and any extraneous costs that might be incurred.

Finding the best items: When it comes to finding the right items to sell, many people automatically think of big-ticket items, under the rationale that, if they can be found on sale, then the profit would be substantial. While these types of items will occasionally pan out, you will almost always find a more reliable return on basic items that everyone needs as they will sell faster and more readily is found for a discounted price. While this isn't the most exciting advice, products like batteries, diapers and ink cartridges are always going to be able to ensure that your retail arbitrage business turns a profit.

While they won't necessarily sell right away, a great type of product to consider selling is seasonal items such as Halloween or Christmas decorations. These items can typically be picked up for pennies on the dollar in the days immediately following the holiday and if you are willing to wait almost a year to sell them, will always return a reliable profit, especially if you wait to a week or so before the holiday to post them for sale. The downside with this being you only have a limited window in order to ensure that the item sells or else you have to hold onto it for another entire year.

Another good choice is to keep your ear to the ground when it comes to new trends and then purchase a large amount of the new hot item in bulk before the price catches up to its new level of popularity. For example, these days' kids are all about fidget spinners that have led the price of many versions of this product to increase dramatically. If you had hopped onto the fidget spinner bandwagon early on, then you could now sell them for a significant profit.

Finally, items from the dollar store that feature popular licensed characters such as Disney princesses or Marvel superheroes are always going to be able to turn a profit. While these products might not sell for much more than their purchase price at the moment, if you wait until a specific product is hard to find, typically four to six months, then you can easily sell it for five times what you paid for it to parents who are desperate for new content for their child who has already consumed everything else with their favorite character's face on the box.

Additional concerns: Outside of just looking for the best deals, give special attention to how a given item is likely to ship before buying in bulk. Keeping this factor in mind will make it easier to prevent a rash of returns on products that are exceedingly fragile or are otherwise difficult or exceedingly costly to ship. Furthermore, you will want to avoid items that are going to be complicated to ship as, if things go well, you will be shipping them out on an exceedingly frequent basis.

With these types of items, a good rule of thumb is to only move forward with sales that will net you at least 50 percent profit on the sold item. The only exception to this rule is if you have a specific idea in mind for the product when you purchase it and don't mind making less from it overall.

eBay to Amazon arbitrage: If you are looking to get into arbitrage without having to purchase any physical product, then you can actually play eBay and Amazon against one another. Specifically, what you do is spend time searching both eBay and Amazon for specific items and then, once you find a product that is selling for more on eBay, simply post a new auction and then, once it ends, purchase the product on Amazon and send it to the winner of the auction as a gift. While Amazon currently frowns upon this, it is not, strictly speaking, breaking any laws.

When it comes to completing this type of arbitrage sale successfully, it is important to ensure that the items you choose aren't on sale on Amazon for an exceedingly limited time as once an auction has been won it is difficult to get out of sending an item, even if you aren't going to make any money for it. Additionally, it is important to always only post a single auction at a time. Not only will this prevent you from losing money if the price changes on Amazon, but it will also make the buyer more likely to pull the trigger because of the apparent level of scarcity that having only one option provides.

Ratings

Profitability - You are directly selling products the way traditional stores do. So the income you earn is mostly direct income.

Perspective in the future - You can easily scale the business by adding more products in your eBay store.

Difficulty - The business model is really simple. Buy products from retail stores then list them for sale at a profit on eBay.

Chapter 7 Cryptocurrency

If you haven't heard about cryptocurrencies, then you have probably been living under a rock for the last decade or so. Just kidding. Cryptocurrencies have taken the online economy by storm. Just a few years ago Bitcoin, the very first digital currency, was introduced to the world. Today, a single Bitcoin is worth more than $6000. Bitcoin was a huge success that other digital currencies like Litecoin and Ethereum were able to rise in value and influence. Now, you can generate a nice income by trading and investing in digital coins.

There are three main ways on how you can make money from cryptocurrencies. One, buy and trade them. There are several cryptocurrency exchanges out there that can facilitate such transactions. Two, you accept cryptocurrencies as payment for specific products and services. And three, you mine your own cryptocurrencies. If you are new in the industry, I suggest that you follow option 1 or 2 or both. Option 3 is just too difficult and/or expensive to pull off these days.

Ratings Based on Our Criteria

1. Simplicity:

Trying to make money from cryptocurrencies if far from being simple. You need to spend time educating yourself on the latest revolution and the intricacies of how they work.

4/10

2. Passivity:

You can make passive income from your Cryptocurrency by lending it to people who will pay you interest on them. There are B2B lending platforms that specialize in helping you lend your Bitcoin e.g. Bitbond, BTCPOP, KIVA etc.

7/10

3. Scalability:

To scale up your earnings, you have to purchase more coins and repeat the steps discussed above.

6/10

4. Competitiveness:

The cryptocurrency industry is already competitive. Expect it to get even more competitive in the coming years as more people warm up to it.

Tips for Success

•   Learn everything you can about the industry before you jump into the bandwagon.

•   Do your research and determine the differences between popular cryptocurrencies like Bitcoin, Litecoin, and Ethereum.

•   Trade only amounts you can afford to lose and only when you have a clear strategy.

•   Always consider the risks and don't be greedy. Look for the smaller profits that can accumulate into bigger profits down the road.

•   Be aware of the fees that are associated with multiple trade actions.

- Don't go looking for crashed coins expecting them to rise in value again.

- Don't put all of your eggs in one basket. Invest in at least two cryptocurrencies.

- Only use cryptocurrency exchanges that have proven themselves to be secure and reliable.

- Use an exchange, not a broker. You'll save a lot of money and time this way.

Chapter 8 Stock Market

Chances come in many ways. Some people say it only knocks once. Others say it lingers. The reality isn't a big deal. It's how you get the chance. Many people will agree that the best opportunity they can have is an income opportunity. That's why everyone searches for it. Yet, it could hardly be noticed by some. It does not necessarily involve much effort to get the chance. The lion is a good analogy. Following ten tries, lions get their prey. They will have used all their food by the time they kill their prey. Your diet is just enough to replace your lost energy, and that energy is just enough to take another day off. On the other side, crocodiles float on the water, wait for their prey, and never let it go. They'll be full and not hungry for a long time after their meal before finding another live victim. The latter is the best example of how to get a shot. And this example is like a passive income incentive in terms of income opportunities.

A careful examination of the economic situation impacting the danger-reward ratio of a specific investment method can be used to consider passive income opportunities. When you invest in the stock market, the right opportunity is if the price of a business you are willing to purchase is at its lowest level. In this case, it is cheap, and the stock valuation value is high. This is another forum for passive income. In the stock market, we benefit from a company's dividends and at the same time, from its appraisal. Taking use of price fluctuations provides some incentives for passive income. Ideally, they buy shares at low prices and sell them at low prices. This also applies to nearly all trading instruments. When a clear and strong pattern emerges, a passive income potential becomes apparent. To make the correct entry, we should understand why these changes take place so that we can monitor the course of the market. The price action of one instrument is essential to know to determine the capacity and limit of a passive income opportunity, and this is determined by the changing market conditions guided by numerous different factors, from which we also have to learn profoundly.

Traders use two methods for assessing a passive income asset, which is known as essential and technical analysis. Fundamental analysis is a tool for analyzing current economic factors affecting consumer behavior.

When the financial situation is excellent, it promises a positive investment growth. Traders are, therefore, ready to buy attractive devices. And by doing this, they force the other market players to raise their prices. But if the economic situation is worse, concerns are triggered, and this is known as an aversion to risk. The latter is referred to as risk appetite.

We can calculate economic strength and weakness using periodic economic indicators. GDP is one of the most famous symbols of the economy. When the GDP number is higher than expected, the economy is stable and investment friendly. The unemployment rate is another important indicator. Consumers are reluctant to spend when the unemployment rate is higher. Industries are struggling. And so, it's a bad investment moment. This is just one example of the importance of each information for traders to make a sound decision. Good economic indicators also provide investors and traders with a passive income incentive.

This economic news can affect the feelings of the consumer. Nonetheless, rumors often make traders respond more than the news. Most traders, therefore, buy stories and sell the news. This is also another area for passive income. How does it work? How does it work? For example, if a company were to launch a highly competitive product, investors would purchase the business a lot earlier. The value of the company would, therefore, also be lower. And if the news isn't real, early purchasers will sell and benefit. Knowledge thus provides us with a passive income incentive.

The use of technical analysis is another approach that traders use to define a passive revenue opportunity. Technical analysis provides traders with historical graph data. The graph may display trends that allow traders to follow the market trend. It also sends a signal that the value of a trading instrument exceeds a certain point where each time a reversal happens. A passive income potential starts when the graph shows a clear trend right after a setback. Experts in this field have various instruments for disclosing a passive income chance. Price is shifting within a trading range here. If the array is disrupted, however, it means a significantly stronger pattern. This is considered a "break-out." A breakthrough event is an excellent opportunity for passive income. The purchasing of an explosion has proven lucrative.

Regardless of whether fundamental or technological approaches are employed, there is always a passive income chance.

There are still other ways of finding passive income, such as new trading instruments. These include the IPO, public bond sales, and any new investment instrument issue. In summary, because it is a new problem, the price is lowest, and there is no way to go up.

The initial public offer (IPO) is a new share problem for the growth of a business. Companies need not borrow money from banks to expand their operations. Instead, they would search for investors to collect their funds to finance the expansion process. The new problem has still not been sold on the stock market. When a company executes the IPO, investment banks buy the new stock issue. Afterward, investment banks will pay for the company. Then the current item purchased by the investment bank will be sold on the stock exchange trading floor. This form of sale in the store is known as an IPO. Why many investors want to purchase an IPO is that most of the businesses that issue an IPO are expanding. When it develops, a company grows, and potential growth is active in the near term. The IPO of a growing company is also sold at the lowest price. The market path is therefore set to a bullish pattern. Those shares will be traded after the initial public offering. Such dividends will become secondary stocks if they are passed from one investor to another. IPO is an excellent example of passive income. Rumors about an IPO increase risk appetite on the stock market. During the economic slowdown, IPO is hardly seen except for the sector to which it belongs. A passive income opportunity begins when the economy is continuously growing, especially if the company that issues the IPO is the primary beneficiary.

Fusion and acquisition also create a passive income incentive because investing in the giant is always enticing.

We saw many possibilities for seeking passive income. If you are still not determined to try one on your own, people who specialize in trading these instruments also have a passive income opportunity. You can ask fund managers for advice. Many high-net-worth people invest in these traders ' proven talents. You can study the way they do about passive income opportunities if you choose to do so. It is also wise to invest in people who already benefit from passive income.

Chapter 9 Option Trading

Options offer an exciting way for investors to get involved in trading. Trading is different than long-term or "buy and hold" investing. Rather than investing in companies in order to build your wealth over a long time period, trading is a method based on using the price movements of securities to earn profits. Most traders seek to earn profits in the near term, the most famous trading method is day trading. In that case, traders open and close their positions within a single trading day.

Trading is often viewed by the public as "gambling". But that perception is not realistic. Traders spend a great deal of time studying the markets, including looking at the fundamentals of the companies they invest in and using technical tools to forecast future price movements. There is a certain probability of success with different trades, but that does not compare to gambling, it is not like spinning a slot machine and hoping lady luck smiles on you. You are not going to be making random options purchases.

The word "trading" can be a loaded term. I will use trading and investing interchangeably because in my view many of the differences are technicalities. You invest to make money, therefore saying that you are investing in options is a perfectly reasonable way to express it.

In this chapter we will begin by giving a formal definition of what an option is. Then we will get into some specifics that you need to know before you start trading.

What is an option?

An option is a contract based on 100 underlying shares of stock. Each contract fixes the price of the stock at a value called the strike price. Options also expire, they come with an expiration date which is sometimes referred to as the expiry.

There are two types of options. These are known as call options and put options. A call option gives the buyer the right to buy 100 shares of stock at the strike price. The contract is called an "option" because buying the shares is optional for the buyer. This is advantageous for the buyer if the market price of the stock rises above the strike price. That way they could save money by being able to get the shares at a discount. This is where an option gets its value.

The higher the market price, the more valuable the option becomes. Of course, if the strike price is above the market price, a call option is not worth nearly as much. But if the share price rises, they will gain in value.

A put option gives the buyer the right to sell 100 shares of stock at the strike price. So, a put option is a contract that gets its value from declining share prices. The way this works is that the investor buys a put option if they believe that future market prices will decline. This fixes the price of the shares. If prices drop by a large amount, they can buy the shares on the open market, and then sell them to the originator of the options contract at the strike price. Since the strike price is higher than the market price, the investor has made a profit.

Options Expire

It is important to focus on the fact that options expire. Time works against an option: the less time on the contract, the lower the probability that market prices will move in the options' favor. This characteristic of options is known as time decay.

If a call option reaches the expiration date and its strike price is below the market price, it could be exercised, which means the owner of the option could buy the 100 shares of stock. This has two advantages. The stock could be immediately sold at the higher market price, earning the investor a profit. Alternatively, if they actually wanted to own the stock, the option gave them the ability to get the shares at a discounted price.

If the strike price is above the market price at that point, the option is worthless, because there would be no point in buying shares of stock at a higher price. In the industry, they say the option expires worthless.

For a put option, on the date of expiration, it's considered valuable if the strike price is above the market price. In that case, the investor can exercise the option by selling the shares of stock at a price that is higher than the market price, earning a profit.

Put options can also be used in an alternative way. Some investors that hold a large number of shares may buy put options as a form of insurance. This can protect them from a catastrophic loss if the stock undergoes a significant decline in price. A put option provides a safety valve they can use to protect their shares.

If the strike price of a put option is below the market price, it expires worthless. An investor is not going to opt to sell shares when they would sell for less than market price.

Pricing definitions

The relationship between option price and market price falls into one of three categories. These are:

- At the money: this means the option strike price is exactly equal to the share price.

- In the money: this means the strike price is favorable with respect to the market price. For a call option, that means the strike price is below the market price. For a put option, that means the strike price is above the market price.

- Out of the money: this means the strike price is unfavorably positioned. For a call option, that means that the strike price is above the market price. For a put option, that means the strike price is below the market price.

Most Options Are Not Exercised

About 85% of options expire worthless. The exact number quoted varies, but the only thing you need to know is that three quarters, or more, of options expire worthless.

There is some mythology about this – people think that because most options expire worthless, they are not exercised. In fact, if an option is in the money the probability that it will be exercised is non-trivial. It constitutes a risk only if you are the originator of the contract. As a trader of options, someone who is buying and selling them on the market, that is not of concern.

Option Price Quotes

Options are quoted on a per share basis. Therefore, you will see an option price listed as $0.74, although that is not the actual price that you will pay for the option. This is a per share quote, and most options cover 100 shares of stock. The actual price that you will pay for an option is the quoted price x 100. In this case, that would be $0.74 x 100 =$74.

Option Lifetime

As a general standard, options last a month. Options typically expire every Friday, but some expire on Wednesdays. There are also weekly options that expire within one week of issue. You can also get long term options that last anywhere between several weeks to 1-2 years. If they last a year or longer, they are called LEAPS, which stands for Long-term Equity Anticipation Security. All options have the same characteristics and behave in the same way, the only difference between them is the length of time to the expiration date.

Writing, Buying, and Selling

Many beginners get confused by the different roles that traders can play in the market. Most investors involved in options are simply trading. This means that you buy an options contract to open your position. You can choose to buy a call option, a put option, or a combination of call and put options. When you buy an option contract you have no obligations under the option, and you are free to sell them to others. In the same way, on the stock market, you don't actually make a deal with someone to sell your option, you simply place an order through your broker, and they handle it for you. Traders buy and sell options hoping to make profits from the transactions as the share price moves up and down. If you get stuck with an option that is out of the money and close to expiration, you are out of luck at that point and it will probably expire worthless.

You can also sell to open. For example, you will be obligated to if the option is exercised by the buyer. Using industry jargon, we say that you have been assigned. They say you are a "writer", but you don't actually write a contract as an individual investor. You simply get on your brokerage contract, and you find existing options for a given stock. When you find one you like, you place an order to sell it through your broker. People sell options because they can earn a monthly income by doing so, even though selling comes with some risks.

Maximum Financial Risk

If you buy options, the maximum risk to you is the money you paid to buy the option. So, if you buy an option for $100 your risk is $100.

If you sell call options, the risk is that you will have to sell the 100 shares of stock. If you own the stock the risk is that you will lose the shares. If you don't already own the stock, then you face financial risk. The risk per share is the difference in price between the market price and the share price.

If you sell put options, the risk is that you will have to buy the shares at the strike price. So, your total risk is the strike price x 100 shares. That is the absolute financial risk, of course you might be stuck with shares of stock that are worthless. As we will see, there are ways to protect yourself from having to buy the stock.

Pros and Cons of Options Trading

Just like anything else, there are pros and cons that come with trading options. The concept sounds great, and in my opinion it is, but options carry risks as well as rewards. It's important to be familiar with both.

First, let's review the advantages. As we have noted, options allow you to get in the market with a far lower amount of capital up-front. If you actually buy shares of stock, it can cost you 20-50 times as much as an options contract would cost.

The second advantage is that options can earn you a much higher return on your investment. Let's say you are a "swing trader", which is someone that buys stock with the hope of earning a profit on a price swing over a short time period. If you buy 100 shares of IBM at $141 a share and the price of the stock goes up by $3 a share, when you close your position you have made $300 profit, minus commissions. Your initial investment would be $14,100. On the other hand, if you buy an option, you can invest $410 and earn a profit of $150. So, you could have made the same $300 profit in absolute terms buying two options, only having to put $820 up-front. You can do the maths to find out how much profit you would make if you put the same amount of money into both investments. On many trading platforms, options trade commission-free.

Another advantage of options is the expiration date, although it is also a liability. Options are a way to make money quickly. You get in, and you get out of your investments.

Options offer leverage. For each options contract you buy, you control 100 shares of stock without actually owning them.

If you buy shares of stock, you benefit if the price rises. You have probably heard about people "shorting" the market, but when it comes to stocks these are big players that have large margin accounts. They have powers that ordinary investors simply don't have, so taking advantage of price declines in the market is not usually something available to small investors.

However, as we noted earlier, put options give you that power. You can short the market for as little as $50 or $100.

Options traders can also create setups that earn profits no matter which direction the stock price moves. That is something you definitely cannot do by owning stocks.

Finally, you can invest in options risking small amounts of capital. That way if you are on the losing end of your trade, the amount of money you lose is fixed and known beforehand.

So, these are the main advantages you get investing in options. If there were no negative sides to it, everyone would be investing in options and becoming millionaires. The reality is options trading can be tricky, and if you don't do it right you will just lose money.

The first disadvantage is that options prices can move fast. The price of an option can double or triple over the course of a couple of hours, and it can also decrease over a short time span. If you are not paying close attention to your trades, you might lose an opportunity to make profits or find yourself with losses in the blink of an eye. In my early trading days, I experienced both outcomes.

Secondly, while the expiration date can be a positive, it is also a major risk factor. One mistake beginners make is not paying attention to the expiration date. If an option is out of the money, it can lose value extremely quickly in the days leading up to expiration. If you are not paying attention and fail to get out of the trade, you can find that prices drop so fast it is not worth bothering.

The next disadvantage is options training can be complicated. I don't recommend just diving in to see what happens. You need to educate yourself before you start trading: start with small trades so that you learn the ropes without investing a large amount of capital. The concept of put options is a little bit foreign to most people, so it should be studied before you start buying.

Chapter 10 Dividend Investing

The idea of dividend investing is considered one of the best ways for investors to collect steady and consistent returns. There are several people who invest in these dividend stocks to take advantage of that dependability before utilizing some of those incoming funds to invest back into more shares of stocks. It is kind of like playing with some house money after winning a few rounds of blackjack at the casino. The main difference is that if you make smart investing decisions, you'll have a better chance at yielding some gains than beating the dealer. Because there are many dividend-paying stocks that represent different organizations that are considered a safer bet for investments. The prices might increase over time, which leads to bigger gains for shareholders. Additionally, those companies will raise dividend payments over time, such as providing a 3 % dividend after one year at about 2.5 %. At the same time, those are never set in stone.

But, a company that builds a profile and gives its shareholders dependable, increasing dividends will do everything possible to continue pleasing their investors.

There are companies that will pay consistently increasing dividends; they are usually considered financially healthy, generating a dependable return on investment on the different dividends. Stable companies usually feature any falling stock prices to make it less alarming for the shareholders in the general market. Because of this, they can be considered less of a risk than the companies that do not pay those dividends and, in turn, see more sharp ups and downs in the price. With a lower risk for the investors of these dividend stocks, they can be a more attractive option for a variety of investors, such as the young bucks who are hoping to get more income over the long haul and for those who are looking to build up their retirement fund. Even those already in retirement use the money from dividend investing in providing a regular income while they are not working. Another reason that these dividend stocks have built confidence among dividend investors is the correlation between the share prices and the yield of gains from the dividends. When one rises, the other follows. There is also the consideration for the power of compounding your investments, which is taking the generated earnings and putting them back into the stocks that will continue to build more and more.

In other words, the money you have generated from your earnings will generate additional earnings, and the generated earnings will continue to multiply as the investor continues to reinvest in the long run. This process can hypothetically turn one penny into a very large sum of money after about a month. If you take that one penny and continue to double your account every day for 30 days, you could see your money grow from a few cents to a few dollars. Ten dollars becomes $20, which becomes $40, then $80, $160, $320, $640, up to thousands and, eventually, millions. Sure, there are a lot of things that have to happen, and it requires a little luck. But in theory, it can happen, even if it is a bit unrealistic. This is not to say that any investor can expect to see their money grow when they begin to utilize dividend investing. But it shows that money can, and likely will, grow in a process that Albert Einstein once called the eighth wonder of the world. Many who enter the world of dividend investing will see the eventual rise of their rate of return as they continue to reinvest the money that comes in their returns on investment. Let us say that you have 100 shares of a stock that sells at $50 per share. This is an investment of about $5,000. In that first year, the company offers a 2.5 %dividend that provides an income of $125. If the investor continues to see dividend growths of 5 % each year, that $5,000 initial investment will be valued at more than $11,200 after about 20 years. This is with the assumption that there will be no change in the stock price, and there is the reinvestment mentioned earlier.

Now let us have that same company pay a quarterly dividend rather than one that pays annually. That $5,000 investment will grow to a little more than $11,650 in two decades for a gain of about 133 %. Because of the process of compounding, a $50,000 investment can become a $116,500 sum after that same period of time during which there are reinvestments into the dividend folder.

How Dividend Investing Can Fit into Your Retirement Goals

The concept of retirement can be mentally draining. You are already working as hard as you can to provide for your family, and then you have to have money after work.

That is not to say that you are in a career where you have to be forced into retirement, but everyone looks forward to the idea of being able to sit on a porch with lemonade on a sunny day rather than put on a suit and go to a busy office. Alas, to be able to reach that dream, you have to have enough money saved up to live on for years, and many folks use an individual retirement account (IRA), which come in various forms because the right type of investments can lead to building up that stockpile of money. That, in itself, is a challenge that can overwhelm a good number of people. First, let us look more into the Roth IRA that people prefer to use to build toward their retirement goals. These IRAs are savings and investment vehicles that have some tax benefits that are more beneficial than a typical investment portfolio.

While a traditional IRA provides an opportunity for an investor's contributions to be made with income deposited before tax is taken out, those distributions are taxed as any other form of income you that would earn from the 40-hour workweek. But when you consider a Roth IRA, those contributions into the stocks are taxed, and the money that is returned to the investor is free of any taxes. Roth IRAs are usually free of taxes when the time comes to get the return on the investments with income that has hopefully built up over time with the power of compounding interest. This means there is a chance to have dividend stocks in the portfolio that pay well and are not being harvested by the greedy IRS tax people. Sure, you have to pay more to get into the party, but the benefits are too great to pass up. So how does the process of dividend investments fit into your retirement goals? A good, dependable dividend investing plan can be the right choice when looking for a portfolio that can build long-term wealth to eventually provide the income to enjoy retirement without any worries of being able to afford not working. One of the biggest factors that attract some retirement planners is the ability to use the power of compounding interest that is found in dividend investment strategies.

Compounding the interest by reinvesting the money you gain regularly requires being able to have a good starting amount of money to be the initial capital, and then investing it in strong equities and letting the price appreciation to be shared and the dividend payments to grow to the point of providing a good base to live on when you do actually retire. Because you are making your dividend investments through something like a Roth IRA, the earnings from those investments are exempt from any taxes that usually hit the money you earn, in many cases, taking out as much as 30 % between state, federal, and an additional federal withholding tax. That is one of the main reasons that people like to use dividend investing as part of their retirement plans. Since Roth IRAs have these tax-free distributed payouts to the shareholders, those returns are more than just the key contributors to the wealth built up for a person's retirement.

Let us add to the fact that the income that comes from the withdrawals of those dividend returns is tax-free. But these IRAs have one disadvantage—of course, there's always a catch—in the sense that these accounts mandate contributions that come from taxable, earned income. On the other hand, the rewards that come from sticking to the plan for several years of dividend investing within a Roth IRA will outweigh those shorter-term costs that one would have to pay upfront. But is the Roth IRA a perfect fit? Well, there are a number of things to consider when choosing between tradition and Roth IRAs: A traditional IRA provides tax-free contributions, while the Roth IRAs offer tax-free income. Roth IRAs provide an advantage in withdrawal taxes since they are not taxed like traditional IRAs. You cannot take out funds without penalty from a Roth IRA until you turn 59-and-a-half years of age, and the IRA has been established for five or more years. A traditional IRA has the same rule, but the money must be withdrawn before 70-and-a-half before a 50 % penalty. There are no limits on contributions within a traditional IRA, but Roth IRAs have a few restrictions, such as the limit on the number of contributions each year if you make more than a certain level of income. Regardless of which IRA type, you will have until April 15 each year to make up the contributions from the prior fiscal year. Overall, those who expect to be taxed at a rate higher than the current income tax when you are expecting to retire—based on tax bracket levels—consider opening a Roth IRA. In the end, different individuals will have their own needs when it comes to how they plan for their retirement. Not everyone can just start at age 18 or in their early 20s. A lot of it depends on their current and potential financial situations down the road, which can affect whether investing in a Roth IRA is the best option for an individual's retirement plan. One way to help in the decision is to know where a person may end up within the tax brackets when they do decide to retire because the Roth IRA may prevent an opportunity to stay away from the higher income tax rates later on. But whatever decision is made on the type of IRA that will form a retirement plan, the main goal is being able to find the best type of investment strategy that can make those golden years of comfortable and relaxing retirement more achievable, which is easily possible with dividend investing within a Roth IRA.

Chapter 11 Real estate

If you want to earn another form of passive income, entering the real estate industry is a great option because it allows you to scalp the market and earn a high profit off of your trades. For real estate purposes, trading real estate essentially means flipping houses or acting as a realtor and connecting people with their desired homes. There are a few ways that you can do this to make it passive—depending on how you want to approach this particular sector of the industry.

Benefits of Real Estate

Real estate will always be in high demand, and your ability to earn a profit on real estate will always be rich. Typically, the profit earned on real estate reaches up into the tens or even hundreds of thousands of dollars based on how much the value of your property increases from the time you purchased your property. You can also earn a profit instantly, however, without having to wait for the market to change if you shop smart and pay close attention to deals.

How You Earn Money Through Real Estate

One of the easiest ways to earn money through real estate is to purchase homes that are being foreclosed or homes that need basic renovations and fix them up before selling them once again. The quicker you sell these homes, the higher your profit which means that you can earn a significant profit in a short amount of time through this method.

You can also earn money through real estate by connecting with realtors who pay bonuses to anyone who helps them find someone who is willing to purchase or sell a home through them. Hence, if you know of a realtor who is willing to offer a bonus if you find them a home buyer who completes a purchase through them, they may offer you a percentage of the sale or a fixed bonus for introducing them to the client. These types of deals are not uncommon, and all they require for you to claim them is to send plenty of customers in the direction of the realtor. This can be a quick and easy way to earn a profit without ever having to purchase or sell real estate yourself.

Getting Started With Real Estate

If you want to get started with real estate, you are going to need to have a fair amount of money saved up to invest in the process from day one. This is how you can ensure that you are going to have enough to invest in a piece of property and earn a profit off of it early on. The only exception to this rule is if you are simply going to be referring paying clients to realtors who are offering bonuses, in which case you just need to build a strong connection in your network and search for people interested in buying or selling homes.

Flipping Fixer-Uppers

If you are going to be regularly purchasing and selling properties that require renovations, you are going to need to get hooked up with both a realtor and a team of people who are capable of fulfilling renovations for you. These people will be able to help you buy the best homes and flip them for as inexpensive as possible. Make sure that you choose a team of people who are highly qualified, but who will also not cost too much so that you can avoid incurring too many expenses in the process. The more you can save during the flip, the more you will earn when you sell the house once again.

Aside from having the right team in place, you also need to have a plan around what types of homes you want to be buying, and where. You will need to be purchasing homes in popular neighborhoods and having as quick of a turnaround time as possible. That being said, if you are not careful you may end up buying a fixer-upper for too much and not being able to turn a high enough profit from the house. For that reason, look for the best deals in the most popular areas, but do not be afraid to look around the outskirts of those popular neighborhoods, too. Many times, people who cannot afford to live directly in a nice neighborhood will look in surrounding areas, which means that they are still prime areas for finding suitable buyers and selling the home quickly.

Avoid choosing homes that are too far outside of these neighborhoods or that are in areas where no one is really purchasing homes. You will end up holding on to these homes for much longer, which will drastically reduce your profitability.

Flipping Foreclosed Houses

Another great way to make a profit through real estate is by purchasing foreclosed homes at a fraction of the going rate and flip them for a profit. There are many specialty websites that exist that can support you in finding local foreclosures and purchasing them for an incredibly reduced rate. These are particularly great purchases because, as long as you are cautious, you can purchase a home that is perfectly fine and that has little to no renovation requirements. A simple cleaning is enough to prepare it to be sold once again—meaning, you can turn it almost immediately. In many cases, if you purchase properly, you can buy these properties and flip them for 1.5x to 2x their purchasing price, which means that you can earn a massive profit.

It is important that you pay attention to any local laws around foreclosures because, in some cases, there may be legal constraints around the house that can prevent you from selling it or that can eat into your profits. Make sure that you are clear on every single deal you enter to avoid getting dinged on unexpected costs and losing out on potential profits through your flipping project.

If you really want to earn a high profit, consider combining both flipping fixer uppers and flipping foreclosures to earn as much as possible. In this case, you want to purchase foreclosed houses that require a fair bit of renovations in order to be ready for resale. By taking an inexpensive foreclosed house and putting some incredible finishing touches on it you can really drive the price up and help get yourself a greater profit, which means that your investment is even more worthwhile in the long run.

It is important that you look for foreclosures in fairly popular neighborhoods, too. Just because you paid less for the property does not mean that you want to pay more to hold onto the house while you wait for a buyer to become available, as this will only eat into your profits. Your opportunities to purchase foreclosures in higher quality neighborhoods may not be as frequent as in other areas, but they will prove to be more profitable in the long run so they are well worth waiting for.

Supporting Other Realtors

If you do not want to get directly involved in real estate but you do want to earn profits from selling homes, you can always get involved by supporting local realtors who offer bonuses to individuals that introduce them to purchasing or selling clients. Many newer realtors or newer real estate offices are looking to increase the number of clients working through them and are willing to pay a finder's bonus to anyone who supports them in finding new clients to support their business. In order to earn that bonus, you simply need to introduce your contacts to the realtor and have them either complete a sale or purchase through the realtor. Once they have, that realtor will pay you a bonus for your introduction which results in you making easy cash just off of a referral.

If you are looking for a way to increase your funds, this can be a great opportunity to keep in mind. While it may not earn you as much right away or be as consistent or reliable, it is still a great way to increase your easy profits in no time at all. You can also improve your odds of earning the bonus by increasing your network and outright asking your friends and family if anyone knows of someone who is looking to buy or sell real estate in the local area. Make sure that your connections are local as most realtors cannot conduct real estate transactions outside of their jurisdiction.

Chapter 12 Domain Flipping

Domain flipping has existed for long as a way of making money on the Internet. Since the dot com era, lots of savvy Internet entrepreneurs have cashed in on the business of domain flipping. Understanding how domain flipping works is quite easy. It is the understanding of how the market works that gets you the real money.

Buying a domain at a low price doesn't mean you will sell it for a higher price. You might fail at it if things are not laid out well. The important thing to consider when going into this business is the market. How do you market your domain?

Before we proceed, allow me to show you just how profitable it is to flip domains. There have been major milestones surpassed in domain flipping. Some domains have sold for over $30,000,000. The website Marijuana.com sold for $8,888,888 in 2011 on heels of the mainstream cannabis adoption. But that's not all. There are regular domain auctions on www.flippa.com, an online website and domain auction platform.

Getting Started

Over 300,000 domains are being registered daily and this comes to about 109,500,000 registered domains a year. Looking at these numbers tells you that there is a huge market for domain flipping.

This is the catch: Most of the domains registered yearly don't get to live past their first year. Oftentimes, once they expire, they are abandoned.

This is the business: These expired domains can be bought by you for pennies on the dollar and then sold for hundreds if not thousands of dollars. Because new businesses are always looking for popular domains, you can cash in on this and make some good money for yourself. Your responsibility is to find good domains, make them yours for cheap and then sell to eager buyers.

Finding the Right Domain

Finding the right domain to purchase for flipping is essential to your success in this business. I will provide the best five factors to consider and the tools to help you make a successful decision. It is important that you know how to judge the quality of a domain and its value.

These are some of the factors to consider when getting your domains:

Consider DOT COM (.com) Domains Only: You should invest only in .COM domains. This is an ideal domain for businesses. Most customers assume the domain to be a .com when told the web address. This is also the domain extension with the highest resale value. Over 50% of all domains sold are .com extensions. You can even leverage your name by purchasing other link extensions and link them to your .com extension.

Pick an Easy Name: The name should be easy to remember and pronounce. Most people have a better affinity with 2 – 3 syllable domains, although this is not the norm and all I am saying is avoid unnecessarily long names, like names with hyphens or numbers. Keep it short and simple.

Look out for Branding: You will have to be a little creative here. Names that sound like brands sell faster and attract more value. For instance; consider a name like cookieJar.com, this name sounds brandable. This is not difficult to do, just think about it a little and it will come to you. Businesses are looking to pay thousands for names that sync with their brand. Sometimes, it is the domain name that gives them an idea of what to call their business.

Keywords Only: This involves finding names that match specific niches. Someone setting up a medical business would want something along the lines of medicine. Domain names that are keywords, or are keyword related, sell faster and have good value.

The Right Value of the Domain: This is the most critical point in finding the right domain. If you make a mistake here, you could lose a lot of money. The value of a domain lies in the number of its backlinks, its relevance and quality. The more backlinks a domain has, the more powerful and valuable it becomes. The position of the backlinks is also important as backlinks within the content matters more. There are several tools online that will determine this, including the Moz site explorer.

When purchasing domains, make sure that the domains are of good quality, and although the earning potential may be huge, you can still get a loss sometimes if you don't apply the right strategies.

Chapter 13 Artistry/Creativity

They use their imaginations to make things that we need on a day to day basis. They may not have enough money to advertise, but they still want to make a living from their ideas. This chapter is meant for anyone that uses their imagination to make anything.

How to Earn a Living as An Artist or Creative

1. Stock Photography

Some people don't know that you can sell your photographs online to people. They assume that you can only get money by getting clients to pay for your skills. There are many people out there that take photos of buildings, plants, animals or landscapes that are not paid by someone to do so. They enjoy the work and would like to know how they can make more money from their photos. There are websites online that buy photographs from talented photographers. Depending on the site, the photographer can be offered a commission every time someone pays to use the photo, or the website can just give the photographer a one-time fee, and they now own the photo. If you have those beautiful pictures of your phone or DSLR camera and don't know what to do with them, you can create a portfolio and approach one of these websites, e.g., Shutterstock. Other sites include Alamy, Picfair, EyeEm, Foap, iStockphoto, Dreamstime, Free digital photo Getty Images, etc. Even if you get a commission from the website, you have no control over what the person who is licensed by the website does with it. Paying you a commission is the better deal as you will be receiving online payments as long as people use your work. How can you have your work approved by one of these websites?

- Have a theme for each photo you take and choose the best from each theme. They only need the best shot; otherwise they could reject your work because of duplication. Keep your submission to 10 photos.

- Some websites have millions of photographs, and they have different categories for each one of them. It is already hard to get in one of these websites, but it is even harder if you submit a photo in a popular category. Do something unique that they may not have seen before, and you are guaranteed to be accepted. Keep your best materials for later and start with a simple yet beautiful shot.

- Avoid submitting photos that capture brand names or trademarked items. That would cause your photo to be rejected for copyright infringement. Avoid people's faces, public places or commercial objects. You may submit them in the future if you're accepted.

- Keep your images the recommended size. Ensure that they are visible and meet the standards of the website you are submitting to.

- Edit your photo before submitting. Many software allows you to do so. You can remove vignettes, add color among other things. Never submit photos with lens flares.

2. Licensing your art to third parties

Here, you have to look for people who need your art say a photograph, music, application and sell them a license to use your product for your work. You will earn more money this way as you are the one that gets to set a price for what you think your work is worth. You will need to have a unique product and look for people that you think can buy a license for it. There are many ways to do that, i.e., through social media, email lists and sending out proposals. Don't just wait for people to stumble upon your work. You can market your work anywhere on the internet where you can reach more people faster. You get to make money licensing the product every time they renew the license while you still get to keep your product.

3. eBooks

We have talked about self-publishing and selling eBooks before in this book; therefore I shall skip through this. Although I should remind you that the book should be based on what you are doing. You can do an introduction of what you so and then be creative with your content. You can make an instruction guide or any other information you may have to share with your reader.

4. Start a Blog Related to your Art

Any business out there is required to have a website in this day and age, so should you for your art. For people to take you seriously, they need to see your portfolio or sample of what you can do before they are convinced to buy. Having a blog also allows you to apply other passive income generating avenues such as advertising, affiliate marketing, email marketing and selling your art online. You can also create a membership site that you can share with your paying audience special work and your process. You make a monthly income as opposed to making them buy something just once. You will require to do more work of creating new products to keep the members satisfied, and you will need more sophisticated software to maintain your site to manage payments and ease of use by users. Despite the workload, you will definitely earn more this way than all the other methods.

5. Make Money by Selling Social Media Shout-outs to other Smaller Artists

If you have a good following on social media, you can make money by approaching smaller talented artists and ask them if they would pay for a shout out. Some will agree, and some may not have the money to pay you so it's up to you if you can help out someone talented by using your platform for good. It is important to remember that you should only be giving shout-outs to people in your niche. You don't want to confuse your audience by introducing a different niche in your space unless it's a collaboration that is tied somehow to your niche.

6. Be a Part of an Artist Collective

It is always better to share ideas with fellow artists than going about it alone. Most people feel the need to try and make it on their own when it can be easier as a group. Artistry, for example, is one of those industries that wouldn't work properly if people failed to communicate and inspire each other. Rather than struggle as a starving artist, link up with other artists that can help you sell your product or art. With people doing similar things or even different things but in the artistic industry, you can come up with cool projects you can do together. You can start art galleries, and you can make niche groups or clubs. You and a group of your similar minded friends can look for ways you can benefit the community you live in through youth projects, teaching classes to the needy and help inspire more people to join the arts.

How to Make an Online Course and Make Money Selling It

The reason I have not included this topic of creating and selling your own online course as a way to make a passive income as an artist is that it is the main way for an artist to make money. The only thing an artist really has is the talent and what better way to leverage that talent than to package it and sell it online. Multiple platforms allow an artist to do that but before then let's look at how to create an online course.

1.   Find a Subject Matter

You already identified the skill that you have and want to share with the world. It's time to look at it in-depth and see if you have enough material to fit an entire course. You will have to come with some interesting materials that people would be interested in paying you for. Create a title that includes the core skills your course will impart on your students. In your description ad two or three more core skills that you promise they will leave with after they complete your course. These are what will enable you to plan your lessons, make marketing easier and deliver your point across to your students.

2.   Find Out if there is a Need

This is important because if people are not interested in the topic you want to teach, then there is no need to do it at all. This is where you can look at what people are saying online and find what else you can include in your course. You need to start learning more about our course so that you are not caught unaware when questions start coming in.

3. Make a Teaching Plan and Course Outline

You have to consider your time and when you are available for the lessons. Talk to your community online and ask them when they are free to take your course and plan around that. You then have to think of how to structure your lessons. Are they in modules or weeks? What should each module contain and how can I make it as interactive as possible? How long are each module and the course in general? Make sure you cover all the bases before you dive in.

4. Consider your Teaching Methods.

Each student is different, and you might want to cater to their different learning styles. Some learn from looking at pictures while others like working on the lessons through a quiz at the end. You can look for feedback to find the best delivery method like text, video, guides, audio, worksheets, etc. You can combine two methods to teach your course.

5. Make your Content

This s where the bulk of your work will be. You have to ensure that you deliver something useful to the people who will take your course; otherwise, you will receive a tone of bad reviews. You also have to make the workload easy for them to follow and ask questions when they don't. The videos and audio should be clear for everyone to follow what you are saying. Brand your material attractively so that people know what they are taking. After you finish the work, go through it again and make sure it is good enough for the students. Before you get cocky and think that you have created the best course ever, it's important to remember that everything you have written can be found free on the internet. Packaging your work in a convenient, easy to understand way is what makes people interested in your course. They want to know everything related to your core skills without having to consult other sources.

Here is how to sell your course online:

1. Plan How to Sell the Course

Assuming you already have a website, add the features that you will need to deliver the course to your community. If you don't, start with that. There are multiple plugins especially on WordPress that help you with the selling and delivery of an online course. If you are not skilled in making such a website, you can sell your course on other websites that already offer that service such as Skillshare or Udemy. You will, however, have to share with the website a part of your earnings depending on the sales you make. The advantages of these websites are that you don't have to worry about delivery systems as they take care of selling the course and processing payments. You will have to reduce the cost of your course because the competition can get very steep. You also don't control your work because you are not running the course. There is a better option that combines two of the different delivery styles. You get to control what the content looks like but still maintain the benefits of an online course website. Examples of such websites include Ruzuku and Teachable.

2. Upload your Course Online

Depending on the platform you choose to deliver your course, you will need to customize your course to look appealing to the students. You will have to use visible fonts, an attractive color scheme and your logo for branding purposes. People need to be able to recognize your brand.

3. Marketing

As with everything else in this book, people need to know what you are doing before they come on board. You will need to use multiple social media sites, blog, email list and many other avenues to tell people why they need to take your course. Social media has paid pay-per-click advertising options that you can pay for to reach more people in your niche. It also allows you to see who is interested in our page among other insights that can help you put together a marketing plan that suits everyone on your community. In your marketing pitches, focus more on what the students will get out of the course rather than focusing on selling the course itself. You can tell them what to expect if they take the course. If you have other courses, offer them testimonials that can be verified so that they can believe you. You need to market your work in your community because they already trust you. Selling to strangers is harder because they don't know you and cannot substantiate if you are genuine or not.

4.   Update your Course Often

Things change every day and so is what is in your course. You need to do frequent research to improve your content, adding what you think people may want to know and removing what is already obsolete. Keep going through the links in your course to see if they are still working. You never know if the website you were referring to remove the content or stopped existing altogether. These small details are what separates you from bad reviews.

5.   Collect Feedback

If you are a genuine seller, you will want to follow up with your students to see if they got anything from your work. If they had any problems, it's important to know so that you can solve them in the future. Take their experiences so that you can use them for your testimonials in the future.

6.   You can Create more Content Through the Steps Outlined Above

Advantages of Passive Income for Artists

1.   People get to recognize your work because of the online platform. Gone are the days that artists needed to physically display their work. You even have a greater audience through marketing yourself online as opposed to physical spaces. This means you can make more money.

2.   You get to learn from other people in the same field. People doing the same thing get to meet each other and discuss their methods of earning passive income from their art.

3.   You get to travel the world and still make more art despite where you are. You can communicate with people you are teaching online which is always a plus. No one cares where you are as long as you deliver your product to your subscribers.

Chapter 14 Virtual Assistant

Many professionals and businesses have resorted to hiring virtual assistants on a contract basis so as to save the cost of hiring in-house employees to handle secretarial and clerical tasks. This has made the demand for virtual assistants to be very high and has created a lot of opportunities for Virtual assistants.

First thing first, who is a virtual assistant? A virtual assistant is anyone who provides support services to other businesses or another person from a remote location, their job description is simple but usually vary depending on the client's needs. It may range from simple typing works on the computer, transcription, social media management, making calls, sending emails, setting reminders for your client to managing website and customers of your client.

This means you can be anywhere in the world and work for anyone in the world, it is just like having a personal assistant that is not with you physically but can do all you want him or her to do. Sounds great, right?

Now, you might be wondering that you do not have any experience in it whatsoever so how do you want to go about it? Well, it's no big deal.

Virtual assistants earn a lot ranging from 15$ -100$ per-hour depending on your skills and experience, once you start, you gain experience as you continue. To become a virtual assistant, you need to have basic knowledge about it like what you're getting here, make as many research as you can on it and that is just enough for you to start.

Let's dive into making money as a virtual assistant, this is quite major.

Get the news out

This means you need to choose the right platform to be seen by people who need your service.

Sell your gig on Fiverr, Upwork, Freelancer or any other freelance website. This is a great way to get started as a freelancer, as it gives you direct exposure to individuals from all over the world who are in need of your service. Setting up an account on these platforms is a very simple process to you can complete in few minutes.

Get the news on social media platforms like LinkedIn, Facebook, Instagram and the likes. It is not just about being on this social media platforms but you need to put yourself out there, make everyone know what you are doing and what you can do. You can list a lot of things like:

Email management

Social media scheduling

Blogging

Freelance writing

Graphics designing

Editing

Copywriting

The list can just go on and on because it is endless, this way you would be able to get great clients that would be interested in your particular skill set depending on your own skill.

Create a Website or Portfolio

A great social media presence can only do a little, a website or portfolio would be more comprehensive of who you are as a virtual assistant. You should add the following to your portfolio or website:

Who you are – This is a short introduction of yourself.

What you offer (you can add what you don't!).

Past experience, examples, portfolio (your previous works if you have any).

Current and past clients (the clients you are working with and those you have worked with).

Topics, industry, Organizations and so on.

Current rates or starting rates (your charges).

Testimonials from current clients (recommendations can also be included).

A contact form.

Feedback or comments (optional).

Charge Per-Hour.

It is always better to charge per hour, because you might not be able to know the full time it would take you to complete projects and other services. It could be more or less than what you think but whichever way, when you are paid per hour, it makes your work easier and your time fully accounted for in terms of your pay.

Increase Your Web of Learning

Learning should not stop for you as a virtual assistant, you need to expand your web of knowledge and you can only do this by learning continually. To earn more, expand your skill set, increase your web of learning.

Now you have what it takes to start earning as a virtual assistant today and fulfil your dreams of working and earning from home.

Chapter 15 Online Courses

People love educating themselves, and online courses are an incredible way to do so. In the past 5 years, online courses have become more popular than ever before because they are short, self-lead, and can support people in learning a wealth of information about topics that actually interest them. Creating an online course does take some time up front, but once it is created, you can continue to sell that course for a long period of time—thus making it a highly passive form of income.

Benefits of Hosting Online Courses

The benefits of hosting online courses that are self-lead, which are sometimes called "evergreen courses," are broad. These courses are a great opportunity for you to position yourself as an expert, offer an ongoing income without having to put in any additional work, and cost almost nothing to make. Some people make a massive passive income online by producing a new course every month or every few months and posting it on a platform like Teachable or Udemy and they produce a great income through this. In some cases, people are earning over $100,000 a year just through creating and promoting their online courses.

If you wanted to, you could also host an online course that is done live—with you instructing said course through a platform like Skype or Facebook Live. In this particular circumstance, you could profit off of the live filming of the course by having paid members joining in on the process. Since the course is being held live, you can also charge more for tickets and earn a higher profit off of this first step. Then, you can go on to add the recordings to a course online and sell it to everyone else for slightly less than your live students paid. This way, you earn an even higher profit and the entire process was profitable.

How You Earn Money With Online Courses

Earning money online through courses is essentially the same as selling products online: every time someone purchases one of your courses you profit from that sale. You can easily continue selling as many digital downloads of your course as you desire and continue earning a profit for a long time. You may need to refresh your courses with some updated information or an updated look from time to time—otherwise, you have a great course online that can be sold for years to come.

Getting Started Making and Selling Online Courses

Creating and selling courses online is simple: you make your course, you post it on a hosting platform, and you market it to your desired audience.

Choosing Your Course Subject

Choosing what you want to teach about will ultimately depend on what your expertise is and what is marketable in the online space. A great way to get a sense of what people are looking for in online courses is to go to a platform like Udemy and browse their main pages. These pages will contain a significant amount of information regarding what is popular at the moment and what you will be most likely to earn a profit in. People are looking to online courses for many different types of information these days, from learning about how to design websites or develop video games to learning about how to meditate or how to market their business. You simply need to choose a subject to teach about and design your course!

Creating Your Course

Most online courses feature a variety of different learning tools to help people learn about the particular topic that is being taught on. Courses will regularly feature video content, written content, quizzes, and "homework" or workbooks for people to use as they go through the course. Although it may take longer, developing a few different types of content for your course will ensure that you have plenty to offer for your prospective students when they consider purchasing your course.

If you are particularly skilled in producing one or two types of content but not all of them, you can always outsource some of your content production to a skilled contractor. Again, Fiverr and Upwork are great resources for finding people who can generate workbooks, written content, or other materials for your course.

Choosing Your Hosting Platform

How you host your course will ultimately depend on how much time or effort you want to put into the hosting process. If you want it to be easy and done in a "plug it in and go" type manner, using Teachable or Udemy is your best option. Teachable will be the best option if you want a completely customized and self-branded website that reflects your business and does not show any signs of which hosting software you are using. However, it will cost you more per month in order to be able to use Teachable if you want to develop many courses and access features like instant payouts when people purchase your courses. Udemy is great if you want to have a platform that is plug in and go and if you do not necessarily care about branding your website personally. You can also partner with Udemy in terms of marketing by selecting an option whereby they earn a larger percentage from your sales but they also promote your course to their viewers. This means that you will show up higher on search listings and that you will be promoted across various platforms where Udemy has paid to sponsor posts or advertisements around the web.

If you want to have a more interactive and personalized platform, you might consider hiring a web developer to completely create your own website that is optimized for selling courses. This will cost you more, but if you are confident in your ability to turn a profit it can also give you far more features and be more flexible in terms of allowing you to do other things on your platform as well.

Promoting Your Online Course

After you have designed your course you simply need to promote it! The best way to promote online courses is to use services like Google Ads as this will help you get your course posted in many different areas across the internet. Facebook and Instagram also have great advertising platforms that can be used for you to promote your course to many other people. While you can leverage your social media presence to promote your course, it is not necessary if you do not already have one as most people will not attempt to search you up online when determining whether or not they want to take your course. Instead, they will look at the contents of the course and the pre-existing reviews of how other students have enjoyed the course and how they felt it was valuable in their learning experience.

Chapter 16 Online Survey

Surveys and forms are very important to individuals, brands and firms because it helps them to improve on areas that need improvements on their products and brands. It also helps them to know more about the opinion of various people and this makes their brand and product better. It also helps to increase sales hence help them to make more money. This is why writing reviews are a very lucrative way to make money. While some might pay you in cash, some might give you freebies and there are some that would give you gift cards.

How can I make money from filling surveys and forms?

You can do this by joining legitimate sites that would pay you to fill surveys and forms. However, there are few sites out there that would tell you they would pay you for filling surveys and forms but they are not legit and will end up not paying you.

How can I pick out the sites that just want to fraud me?

A site that looks for honest reviews and not just any article.

Look for the company's privacy policy in their contract. (If you can't find the privacy policy, or if it says something like the company is free to share your information, stay away from that company.)

A site that has a legit way of paying either through PayPal or a check.

A survey company that is asking you to pay up front is a green light to run.

A site that has been in the business for more than 6 months

A list of some sites that are legit has been complied so you can just join them depending on whichever one pays you.

Swagbucks

Swagbucks is one of the most trusted companies for online surveys and forms. Taking online surveys on any kind of topic is one of the highest paid tasks on Swagbucks. You can earn up to 50 – 300 SB's per survey, and surveys have an average of about 20 minutes on Swagbucks.

However, you can get frustrated wasting your time trying to qualify for surveys because surveys are directed at a particular group. Though you would later find befitting surveys but it might just take time. That's another way to earn SB on Swagbucks.

Paid points

Paid points is a trusted website that was founded in 1996. The company offers various ways to earn money and filling out surveys and forms is one of it so you can be sure to earn through filling survey and forms. Whatever you earn can be drawn to gift cards at Amazon, Walmart, and PayPal.

Toluna

This is one of the largest panels with daily online surveys and forms, paid as cash or vouchers. It is another trusted website that is working on behalf of leading companies. You earn points for each survey and you can earn between 2,000 - 50,000 points in a day (80,000 points earns you a £15 voucher). Your earnings can be used or withdrawn through PayPal payments, Amazon and high-street vouchers.

It takes about fifteen minutes to complete a survey, so it will take about four hours overall to earn a £15 voucher.

Pinecone Research

This is a legitimate company with daily online surveys and forms to fill. They pay well; they pay about three dollars per survey taken. It is not easy to join them as they do not always accept new panel members, but you can continue to check back regularly to know when they are accepting sign-ups.

Chapter 17 Network Marketing

It's a method of selling in which the item owner doesn't use the sales force. Instead the earnings are done by those who have their own companies to advertise the product or support of their parent business. They have paid not just for their own earnings but also the earnings of these people they recruit in the company. This is known as creating a non - other small business people who wish to market themselves. The conventional system advertising strategy is to construct a structure of additional business partners and ensure they succeed. The more effective your company partners subsequently the more income you're going to make. The specific structure will differ from company to company depending upon their reimbursement scheme. It's all up to you to make sure that you put partners in the right place in the arrangement to maximize income. He saw that it's a very low cost system which enables anyone to have their own opportunity at a profitable business enterprise. Generally, results are conducive to the effort you're ready to put in the business enterprise. The most prosperous people in network marketing seem to not be people who are excellent salespeople but really they are the men and women that are mentors and teacher for their business partners. In reality, not only do the many prosperous men and women earn money in addition they figure out how to return to society in precisely the exact same time by helping others.

Examples of network advertising operations include excel communications, mary kay, and avon products.

With the ideal network marketing company, one has all of the anyone considering marketing

The simple process of speaking other clients who refer other customers some reputable before making a determination, joining a network marketing operation ought to do their research. Consider these questions:

- was it pitched as an opportunity to generate money by selling products or by recruiting others?
- what's the track record of the organization's founders?
- are you personally enthusiastic about the goods?
- are individuals you know enthusiastic about the products?
- is the product being marketed effectively?

- do you foresee a comparatively speedy pathway to gains or a lengthy time?

- network marketing appeals to individuals with high energy and strong sales skills, who will build a profitable company with a small investment.

- a network marketing business may be single-tier program, whereby you market the merchandise or multi-tier where you recruit salespeople.

- beware of network advertising businesses which create many tiers of salespeople and completely research the company before you join.

Remember, these are services or goods that we are already marketing as our home-based business.

Thus, the earnings the benefits and drawbacks of network attached to the media marketing business, particularly those with many tiers, which can be characterized as pyramid schemes the salespeople at the top tier can make amounts of money on commissions out of the tiers beneath them. The people on the lower tiers will make less. The company makes money by selling new recruits expensive starter kits.

Salespeople rely on product sales as well as recruiting. Those who are in a high tier and got in early make the most.

Are the goods less expensive? Into a network marketing business, presents an opportunity for a redistribution of is related to marketing when you purchase a product or service, usually over 50% of the cost! That would be no cost associated with getting someone to buy the item plus any cost incurred once it's produced by the factory. With network marketing, the products are sent directly to the user from the factory. Those currencies connected with marketing are paid to several home-based network marketing companies owners which had previous network marketing or internet marketing sway in their customer's referral!

Clients will not buy products and there is limited advantage to paying a bit less for a product on the run. Let us assume that you purchased a product, ordered it to yourself and the company paid a 50 percent commission or rebate to you. In effect you've saved 50% on the products you bought. That could save you a couple of bucks. The idea of earning money which we are buying is a lot more exciting, though saving money is important.

Key takeaways purchasing, or ought to be, and this is. In essence, the concept is to redistribute the advertising dollar! A good rule of why consider network what is network marketing? In time, a tier can sprout still another tier, which contributes commission to the individual in the middle grade as well as the top tier.

Imagine using a network of thousands of customers purchasing quality everything instantly. We are however, implying that folks think about the addition of the right home-based network marketing company starting their trip of financial success in a different direction. Possessing a home-based company is not a new concept. Network marketing is not an idea that is new. Possessing a home-based network marketing company isn't a new idea. Never in the history of our nation has the concept been widespread and is fast becoming the standard rather than the exception!

There's some stigma and the motive is quite simple. Our concept is supplying american's with what they need; control of financial chances and the time proportionate to their skills and effort.

Network marketing is that an individual with a great deal of energy and sales abilities can create a company with a modest investment.

That network advertising operations have a tendency to be more reputable than multi-tier strategies.

Benefits and advantages of unlimited financial opportunity and a home-based company generally connected with a large business.

Traditional marketing vs network marketing

A traditional business would normally have a vice president of marketing with many regional supervisors reporting directly into them. Those regional supervisors would recruit, employ, train and handle several area managers that, then, would every recruit, employ, train and handle several sales agents. The sales agents are subsequently responsible for promoting the organization's services or products.

It is quite evident that the higher the level the greater the cover and there is not as much space on top for progress. It's also evident it is mathematically impossible for every sales representative or worker to grow to the top no matter how great a job they do!

The difference first of all, network marketing differs. Each person starts at precisely the exact same amount - in the very top of the organization, has precisely the exact same chance as everyone else and can be paid in right proportion to the action or achievement they have had an effect in creating. Second, one does not have to be a sales man to reap the degree of fiscal benefits usually associated with business owners, sales managers and entrepreneurs. We might also decide to utilize those which we're generating earnings for, since, typically, they do not earn money unless we perform.

How does this function?

In network marketing, you will find clients and also independent agents who function as a home-based small business. The consumers might also be independent reps. Independent reps can make management positions whenever they so want. Different than in conventional company, every independent agent is given the opportunity and obligation of both recruiting clients and other independent agents.

Network promoting marketer describes others who want to be clients and or independent agents (home-based small business owners). The individual rep helps those recently recruited independent representatives build their own home based business by assisting them identify different clients and independent representatives who want to have their own house based network promoting company. In a mature business, it's common for there to be 50-100+ clients for every customer/independent agent that you refer! By means of this duplication and multiplication procedure every home based business operator can recruit and host a few clients and/or independent agents and, consequently, create a large organization of customers and entrepreneurs.

Referring does this seem like a foreign and embarrassing action to you? How many individuals have you ever referred to a favourite restaurant or into your favourite film? Just how many more have gone since the people you informed loved the restaurant or film and told somebody else that travelled? We're all already talking clients every day! It's simply that the majority of us do not get compensated for it.

The question isn't whether we refer clients, the query is if we're getting paid for your action!

"advertising" the goods for the provider by simply referring other clients! Normally, we get reimbursement through 5 - 10 generations of the duplication activity. Additionally, there are normally additional functionality and leaderships bonus payment arrangements! Assuming an institution with the ideal business: network marketing is your among the hardly any procedures I know of the place you may earn in community advertising terms of your skill and effort with almost infinite potential! Even though most individuals are searching just for a few hundred or few thousand of extra earnings, I know, know of, or have fulfilled a significant amount of folks who make a number of thousands of dollars each month out of their home-based network promoting company!

When it's been ascertained that a home-based company is proper, and further decided that a home-based network marketing company is much more suitable, the real problem is in deciding which network advertising chances to become involved in. Without expertise in the market, unless you are extremely lucky, it's near impossible to select a winner on the first attempt! Regrettably, it appears that expertise in the business isn't necessarily sufficient for the appropriate evaluation of a community promoting opportunity. As is true for traditional business, you will find great opportunities and poor chances. As is true for conventional organization, unfortunately many men and women allow their emotions cloud their logical judgement in regards to assessing a community promoting business and/or business chance!

Conclusion

Remember, investing is never guaranteed no matter how conservative your investment portfolio is, so you should always be cautious around how you are investing and what you are investing in. This book is a great resource to help you get started, but I encourage you to really take your understanding and education even further when you decide which type of investment you want to get in on so that you feel confident in that investment. Education truly is the best way to hedge yourself against risks as it cannot take the risk away completely but it can prevent you from making unnecessary mistakes or bad moves and losing your funds off of a simple mistake. You should never stop learning when you get started in investing as this is your opportunity to stay knowledgeable in the latest investing trends and strategies that you can leverage to improve your success.

If you are still unsure as to where you should start, with real estate or with trades, I encourage you to look at how much you have to start with and consider what your goals are. If you have a large amount to invest and you want a long-term investment that is a fairly low risk, starting with real estate may be the best option. While you will not get your principal funds or profits back nearly as fast, it is one of the most secure ways to invest your money and protect yourself against inflation. If you only have a smaller amount to invest and you want to get started right away, consider getting involved in online trading. Creating a diverse portfolio between ETFs which are one of the safest investments for beginners and maybe adding in a few stocks gives you the opportunity to begin earning a profit right away. Then, of those investments, you can reinvest your profits into real estate and start diversifying your portfolio even further. This is a great way to get yourself started and achieve success through your personal investment strategies.

The fact that passive income is a sure way of making extra money doesn't mean that the field remains rigid. You will constantly have to learn what is changing in the industry could make a world of difference in your returns in the long run. Look at trends and what people are looking for, but you still need to add our personality to it to make it even better.

www.ingramcontent.com/pod-product-compliance
Lightning Source LLC
Chambersburg PA
CBHW071405210526
45465CB00001B/261